ADVANTAGE Grammar

Grade 3

Table of Contents

Table of Contents

CREDITS

Concept Development: Kent Publishing Services, Inc.
Written by: Jeff Putnam
Editor: Thomas Hatch
Design/Production: Signature Design Group, Inc.
Illustrator: Jenny Campbell
Art Director: Tom Cochrane
Project Director: Carolea Williams

Introduction

The **Advantage Grammar** series for grades 3-8 offers instruction and practice in key writing skills, including

- grammar and usage
- capitalization and punctuation
- spelling
- writing good sentences
- writing good paragraphs
- editing your work

Take a look at all the advantages this grammar series offers . . .

Strong Skill Instruction

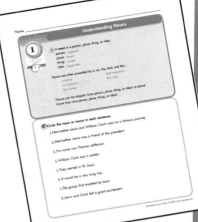

- The teaching component at the top of each lesson provides the support students need to work through the book independently.

- Plenty of skill practice pages will ensure students master essential skills they need to become competent writers.

- Examples, models, and practice activities use content from across the curriculum so students are learning about social studies, science, and literature as they master writing skills.

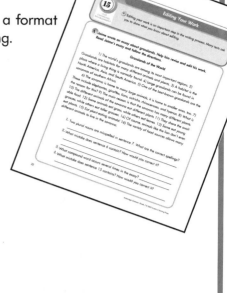

Editing Your Work pages provide for mixed practice of skills in a format that supports today's process approach to the teaching of writing.

Take a Test Drive pages provide practice using a test-taking format such as those included in national standardized and proficiency tests.

Name _____

1

LEWIS AND
CLARK

Understanding Nouns

★ A **noun** is a person, place, thing, or idea.
person: explorer
place: forest
thing: canoe
idea: happiness

Nouns are often preceded by *a, an, the, that,* and *this.*

a forest   that mountain
an explorer   this river
the canoe

Nouns can be singular (one person, place, thing, or idea) or plural
(more than one person, place, thing, or idea).

A **Circle the noun or nouns in each sentence.**

1. Meriwether Lewis and William Clark went on a famous journey.

2. Meriwether Lewis was a friend of the president.

3. His name was Thomas Jefferson.

4. William Clark was a soldier.

5. They started in St. Louis.

6. It would be a very long trip.

7. The group first traveled by boat.

8. Lewis and Clark felt a great excitement.

                                    Advantage Grammar Grade 3 © 2005 Creative Teaching Press

Name _____

B Read the clue. Then write in the correct noun.

1. Native American _person_

2. large, furry animal that lives in a forest _bear_

3. very dry place _desert_

4. tool for cutting down trees _axe_

5. opposite of sadness _happiness_

C Find the 14 nouns in the word search. Write each noun you find on the lines below. Words can be down or across.

```
E C L N O I S E
A O P I A F Z C
G U X G V E A T
L R Q H N A H B
E A S T A R I W
D G U I D E O O
J E H O R S E L
F O R E S T L F
```

Courage _____   _____

Forest _____   _____

noise _____   _____

night _____   _____

fear _____

horse _____   _____

star _____   _____

Understanding Verbs

LESSON

2

LEWIS AND
CLARK

⭐ A **verb** is a word that shows action.

Horses **eat** hay. Hawks **fly** high in the air. Snow **falls** on the mountain tops.

Some special verbs show a state or condition of something.

Apples **are** red, green, or yellow. Martin **is** my cousin.

A **Circle the verb in each sentence.**

1. Lewis and Clark are famous American explorers.

2. St. Louis sits on the Mississippi River.

3. The Missouri River is often very muddy.

4. Our class studies geography and history.

5. Different plants grow in different regions.

6. The wind blows hard just before a storm.

7. I dream about the camping trip.

8. My family recycles paper and plastic.

9. The Missouri River flows from east to west.

10. The Lewis and Clark expedition began in 1803.

11. I like to paddle a canoe.

12. Spending time outdoors is fun.

B Complete each sentence by adding a verb.

1. Montana _____ is a beautiful state.

2. Many wild animals _____ in the Rocky Mountains.

3. To find their way, explorers _____ at maps.

4. They must also _____ many dangers.

5. Nights in the mountains _____ very cold.

C Write a sentence about mountains using each verb.

1. grow _____

_____

2. runs _____

_____

3. camp _____

_____

4. are _____

_____

5. fly _____

_____

Name _____

Phrases and Complete Sentences

⭐ Complete sentences have **subjects** and **predicates**.

<u>Lewis and Clark</u> <u>kept journals</u>.   <u>The great explorers</u> <u>also drew maps</u>.

      subject   predicate   subject   predicate

Sentences sometimes have **prepositional phrases**. A preposition shows how a noun or pronoun relates to other words in the sentence.

<u>Lewis and Clark</u> <u>kept journals</u> **during** <u>their journey</u>.

      subject   predicate   phrase

<u>The great explorers</u> <u>also drew maps</u> **of** <u>their travels</u>.

A **Circle the subject and underline the predicate of each sentence.**

1. Sacagawea was a Shoshone woman.

2. She helped Lewis and Clark.

3. The difficult journey lasted several years.

4. Lewis and Clark became heroes.

5. The two men received important government jobs.

Name _____

B Each sentence contains a phrase in addition to a subject and predicate. Underline the phrase in each sentence.

1. President Thomas Jefferson bought a large amount of land.

2. In 1803, the United States bought the land.

3. The land belonged to France.

4. It included the important port of New Orleans.

5. Jefferson sent Lewis and Clark across the continent.

C Look at the underlined part of each sentence. On the line, write *subject* if the underlined part is the subject. Write *predicate* if the underlined part is the predicate. Write *phrase* if the underlined part is a phrase.

1. Sacagawea was married to a Canadian trapper named Charbonneau.

   _____

2. She journeyed with the explorers for many thousands of miles. _____

3. The group traveled deeper into North Dakota. _____

4. Once, their boat tipped over on the Missouri River. _____

5. Sacagawea gathered all the bags. _____

6. Charbonneau and Sacagawea took their baby on the trip. _____

7. The Native American guide was able to talk to the different tribes. _____

8. Today, her picture is on the dollar coin. _____

Name _____

End-of-Sentence Punctuation

⭐ Every sentence must end with a punctuation mark. A sentence that makes a statement ends with a **period**.

> The Lewis and Clark journey lasted almost three years.

A sentence that asks a question ends with a **question mark**.

> Did they spend the winter in Oregon?

A sentence that expresses strong emotion ends with an **exclamation point**.

> My goodness, they were brave!

A sentence that makes a command ends with a period or an exclamation point.

> Please tell us about Sacagawea.

> Don't touch that snake!

A **Add the correct punctuation mark at the end of each sentence.**

1. There were about 40 people in the Lewis and Clark Expedition _____

2. Do you know what an expedition is _____

3. An expedition is a long trip with a goal _____

4. Were Lewis and Clark both from Virginia _____

5. Yes, they were both Virginians _____

6. Was Virginia one of the thirteen original colonies _____

7. Look out, Captain Lewis _____

8. There's a bear behind that rock _____

9. Don't worry _____

10. The members of the expedition got safely away from the bear _____

B Read each sentence. If the sentence uses the correct end mark, write a *C* on the line. If it uses an incorrect end mark cross out the incorrect mark and write the correct end mark on the line.

1. Did you know that Meriwether Lewis was an expert hunter. _____

2. They hunted game and caught fish during the journey. _____

3. William Clark made most of the group's maps. _____

4. His older brother was George Rogers Clark, a Revolutionary War general? _____

5. Are you surprised to learn that Clark was a good artist? _____

6. His drawings of animals and plants were very helpful to scientists _____

7. Lewis and Clark worked together well! _____

8. Just think of the dangers they overcame together? _____

9. The travelers returned to St. Louis on September 23, 1806? _____

10. Imagine the tremendous excitement! _____

C Lewis and Clark spent much of their journey walking through woods and forests. Write four sentences about a walk in the woods. Use each kind of end-of-sentence punctuation.

_____

_____

_____

_____

_____

_____

_____

_____

Name _____

Spelling One-Syllable Words with Blends

LEWIS AND
CLARK

⭐ Sometimes consonants work together. For example, you know the sound of *p*
in *pig* and the sound of *h* in *hoop*. But when *p* and *h* come together, their
sound is like *f*, as in *graph*. Some other consonant pairs that make special
sounds are

sh   ch   th   ng

Some common words with these pairs are

ship   fi**sh**   **ch**ange   **ch**eek   **th**ink   ba**th**   si**ng**

Ⓐ **Read the clue. Then complete the word.**

1. what a bride gets at a wedding   __ __ n g

2. this comes out of a hen's egg   c h __ __ __

3. the opposite of pull   __ __ s h

4. something you can do with a ballt   h __ __ __

5. a season with flowers and baby birds   __ __ __ n g

6. what you make when you jump off a diving board into the water __ __ __ __ s h

7. a small object that lets you talk to people miles away   p h __ __ __

8. a place where you can swim or catch some rays   __ __ __ c h

9. a little building where you can keep tools, bikes, or other things   s h __ __

10. the opposite of short   __ __ n g

11. put this on a table to catch crumbs and look nice   __ __ __ t h

12. a person who is not yet an adult   c h __ __ __

Advantage Grammar Grade 3 © 2005 Creative Teaching Press

B Circle each word that is spelled correctly.

surch   hange   htank   shoutt

thikc   wing   teech   shape

spring   chooose   boosh   both

C Now write a sentence using each word that is INCORRECT in the list above. Use the correct spelling in your sentences.

_____

_____

_____

_____

_____

_____

_____

_____

_____

_____

_____

_____

_____

_____

_____

_____

Name _____

Spelling Contractions

 Sometimes when we speak, we shorten words by leaving out sounds. For example, you may say, "I **don't** like cabbage," instead of, "I **do not** like cabbage. These shorter, easier words are called contractions. Here are some common contractions and the words they stand for:

aren't (are not)	I'll (I will)	could've (could have)
won't (will not)	she'll (she will)	should've (should
can't (cannot)	I'd (I would or I had)	have)
isn't (is not)	he'd (he would or	shouldn't (should not)
I've (I have)	he had)	he's (he is)
you've (you have)	they'd (they would or	she's (she is)
doesn't (does not)	they had)	it's (it is)
couldn't (could not)	I'm (I am)	you're (you are)
wouldn't (would not)	we're (we are)	they're (they are)

Most contractions include a verb. An apostrophe takes the place of the missing letter or letters. In **don't**, for example, the apostrophe takes the place of the *o* in *not*.

A **Read the sentences. Underline each contraction.**

1. Isn't the Lewis and Clark story interesting?

2. In school, we're reading about their journey.

3. It's Megan's favorite part of U.S. history.

4. They're her two heroes!

5. I think she'd like to go to St. Louis.

6. She could've gone last summer.

7. Lewis and Clark couldn't speak with the Native Americans.

8. Without Sacagawea, they would've been in trouble.

9. You're giving a report today about the expedition.

10. I knew I wouldn't be there to hear it.

B Look at each contraction you underlined in exercise A. On the lines below write the words that each contraction stands for.

1. _____

2. _____

3. _____

4. _____

5. _____

6. _____

7. _____

8. _____

9. _____

10. _____

C Circle the contraction that correctly completes each sentence.

1. (Id'/I'd) like to learn more about the Lewis and Clark expedition.

2. Did you know (they're, there) the subject of a new movie?

3. Have you decided when (your/you're) going to see it?

4. Sean (wouldn't/would'nt) miss the movie for anything!

5. I think (its/it's) too late to go tonight.

D Imagine you are taking a family trip. You are following the route Lewis and Clark took from St. Louis across the Rocky Mountains to the Pacific Ocean. Write a post card or E-mail home to a friend about what you have seen on your trip. Use some of the contractions from the list on page 14.

_____

_____

_____

LESSON

7

LEWIS AND
CLARK

Editing Your Work

 Editing your work is an important step in the writing process. Many tests ask you to show what you know about editing.

 Brian wrote a report about Lewis and Clark's scientific studies. Help him revise and edit his work. Read the first two paragraphs and follow the directions.

A Journey for Science

1) Lewis and Clark had many important goals for their journey. 2) They wanted to discover a water route from the East to the Pacific Ocean? 3) The explorers also hoped to meet the Native Americans who lived in the new territory. 4) In addition, they wanted to set up a fur-trapping industry. 5) Perhaps their biggest responsibility was to study nature.

6) President Jefferson was very interested in plants, animals, mountains, and rivers. 7) He asked Lewis and Clark to takes notes on everything they saw. 8) The list of animals they studied is quite long. 9) You have probably heard of many of them. 10) Some of the animals they studied are the raven, catfish, coyote, harbor seal, mountain lion, and porcupine. 11) The explorers also saw several kinds of beavers, foxes, bobcats, mountain sheep, squirrels, rattlesnakes, deer, and toads. William Clark made drawings of many of these animals.

1. What are the nouns in the first sentence?

_____

_____

2. Sentence 2 has an error. Rewrite the sentence correctly.

_____

3. In sentence 9, there are two words that could become a contraction. Write the words. Then write the contraction.

_____

4. Which two words in sentence 11 have consonant pairs that make a third sound? _____

   Advantage Grammar Grade 3 © 2005 Creative Teaching Press

B Shana's uncle loves to hike and camp. One time he crossed the Bitterroot Mountains in Idaho. He took the same trail that Lewis and Clark did. She wrote this newspaper story about her uncle. Read the first part of Shana's news story. Then answer the questions to help her revise and edit her work.

1) Almost 200 years ago, Lewis and Clark faced their greatest challenge. 2) They were crossing the Bitterroot Mountains in Idaho. 3) It was fall, and the weather was turning cold. 4) The sky was filled with clouds. 5) Could snow be far away?

6) The mountain pass led almost straight down. 7) Their horses could barely keep their feet. 8) A stumble meant a long, terrible fall, even death. 9) Their brave guide, Sacagawea, had a special reason to be afraid. 10) She had her newborn baby with her!

11) Last year, my uncle. 12) Made the same trip. 13) He wanted to hsare the dangers that Lewis and Clark faced. 14) Here's his story.

1. Sentence 2 contains a phrase. Write it here.

_____

2. Sentence 13 has a word with a blend that is misspelled. What is the correct spelling?

_____

3. Which sentence expresses strong emotion and ends with the correct punctuation mark?

_____

4. Two sentences in the story are not complete sentences. Which ones are they? Rewrite them as one complete sentence.

_____

5. Which sentence contains a contraction? What words does the contraction stand for?

_____

_____

Name _____

Take a Test Drive

Fill in the bubble beside the correct answer.

Mandy wrote a report on Thomas Jefferson and his ideas about the West. Help her revise and edit her report. Read the report and answer the questions that follow.

1) Thomas Jefferson was a very smart man. 2) However, the third president held many of the beliefs of his time. 3) You can see this in some of his orders to Lewis and Clark.

4) For example, he wanted them to look for certain things on their journey? 5) Jefferson expected the explorers to find a water route through North America. 6) Many people believed that you could travel by boat from the Atlantic to the Pacific. 7) Lewis and Clark found out that this wasn't true. 8) Jefferson also asked them to look out for llamas and even wooly mammoths. 9) These elephant-like creatures became extinct 10,000 years ago!

10) The president had also heard about the Native Americans in the West. 11) He asked Lewis and Clark to see if they really spoke Welsh. 12) Welsh was the language of Wales, a small country next to England. 13) None of these beliefs was true. 14) But Lewis and Clark discovered many wonderful things about the West, anyway.

1. Which statement is true about sentence 2?
   Ⓐ *president* is the verb.   Ⓒ *held* is the verb.
   Ⓑ It has no phrases.   Ⓓ It is not a complete sentence.

2. Sentence 9 ends with an exclamation point because it expresses which strong feeling?
   Ⓕ anger   Ⓗ sadness
   Ⓖ amazement   Ⓙ fear

3. Which statement is false?
   Ⓐ Sentence 3 has an incorrect end punctuation mark.
   Ⓑ In sentence 10, the word *president* is the subject.
   Ⓒ Sentence 7 is a complete sentence.
   Ⓓ Sentence 11 is a complete sentence.

4. What change is needed in sentence 4?
  - Ⓕ Make it a complete sentence by adding a subject.
  - Ⓖ Make it a complete sentence by adding a verb.
  - Ⓗ Change the question mark to a period.
  - Ⓙ Change nothing—it is correct.

5. Mandy has decided not to use contractions in her report. What change should she make?
  - Ⓐ Change *wasn't* to *was not* in sentence 7.
  - Ⓑ Change *wasn't* to *was* in sentence 7.
  - Ⓒ Change *none* to *not one* in sentence 13.
  - Ⓓ Change *none* to *no one* in sentence 13.

6. How should sentence 9 be changed?
  - Ⓕ Make it a complete sentence by adding a subject.
  - Ⓖ Make it a complete sentence by adding a verb.
  - Ⓗ Change the exclamation point to a question mark.
  - Ⓙ Change nothing—it is correct.

7. Which statement is false?
  - Ⓐ The word *elephant-like* in sentence 9 is not a contraction.
  - Ⓑ Sentence 1 has correct end punctuation.
  - Ⓒ *Wales* is the subject of sentence 12.
  - Ⓓ A prepositional phrase in sentence 13 is *of these beliefs*.

8. Which of the following is a prepositional phrase?
  - Ⓕ *from the Atlantic to the Pacific* in sentence 6
  - Ⓖ *a very smart man* in sentence 1
  - Ⓗ *Many people* in sentence 6
  - Ⓙ *10,000 years ago* in sentence 9

Name _____

Singular Nouns

 A noun is **singular** when it refers to only one person, place, thing, or idea. The words *a*, *an* or *the* often come before singular nouns.

ranger   bird   leaf   pond   excitement

a scientist   a penguin   the ocean   an orange   the anger

 A **Underline each singular noun.**

1. Penguins live only south of the Equator.

2. Some, but not all, penguins live at the South Pole.

3. Many people enjoy learning about this interesting bird.

4. Penguins fit well into their environment.

5. Its coat of feathers is very dense.

6. They keep the penguin warm in cold weather.

7. Its wings work like flippers, moving the bird through the water.

8. The shape of its body also helps the bird swim.

9. One kind of penguin can swim 22 miles an hour!

10. The largest penguin can weigh almost 70 pounds.

B Look at the underlined singular noun in each sentence. On the line write *person, place, thing,* or *idea* to tell what the noun names.

1. Each region of the <u>earth</u> contains plants and animals not found anywhere else. _____

2. Ecology is the study of <u>plant</u> and animal life. _____

3. An <u>ecologist</u> studies the health of the environment. _____

4. The forest, the sea, and the <u>desert</u> contain different plants and animals. _____

5. Scientists express fear that the <u>environment</u> may be seriously damaged. _____

C Write a paragraph about a region of the earth you would like to visit. Underline each singular noun in your paragraph.

_____

_____

_____

_____

_____

_____

_____

_____

_____

_____

Name _____

Plural Nouns

 Plural nouns refer to more than one person, place, thing, or idea. Most plural nouns are formed by adding -s to a singular noun.

workers   oceans   boats   freedoms

Singular nouns that end in -sh, -ch, -s, -ss, and -z form their plurals by adding -es. So do most nouns that end in -o.

bushes   churches   gases   guesses   buzzes   volcanoes

When a singular noun ends in a consonant followed by y, change the y to i before adding -es.

baby—babies   cry—cries   lady—ladies

Some special plural nouns add an ending other than -s or -es or have the same form for singular and plural.

child—children   fish—fish   deer—deer

Some singular nouns change vowels or consonants to make their plural forms.

man—men   woman—women   mouse—mice
foot—feet   leaf—leaves   wolf—wolves

A Underline each plural noun. Some sentences may not have a plural noun.

1. Many animals are cold-blooded.

2. Snakes, turtles, fish, and alligators are all cold-blooded.

3. These creatures take in heat from outside their bodies.

4. They cannot stay warm if the weather turns cold.

5. That's why many of these animals hibernate, or sleep, during winter.

6. Many make nests in dry leaves, caves, or holes in the ground.

7. One of the largest cold-blooded animals is the komodo dragon.

8. Men and women who study animals are called zoologists.

Advantage Grammar Grade 3 © 2005 Creative Teaching Press

B Write the correct plural for each singular noun.

1. knife _____

2. sheep _____

3. sky _____

4. hutch _____

5. reptile _____

6. hero _____

7. day _____

8. child _____

9. mess _____

10. potato _____

C Circle the word that correctly completes each sentence.

1. Some warm-blooded animals can live in the earth's coldest (regions/regiones).

2. The have developed different (wayes/ways) to stay warm.

3. For example, (musk oxs/musk oxen) have thick hair coats with two layers.

4. They also have especially large (hoofs/hooves), which do not sink into the snow.

5. These animals cluster together in large (groupes/groups) for warmth.

Name _____

Sentence Fragments and Run-on Sentences

⭐ A **sentence fragment** is an incomplete sentence.

The first sentence below is missing its predicate. The second is missing its subject:

> The largest member of the deer family. Is the moose.

To make a complete sentence, combine them:

> The largest member of the deer family is the moose.

A **run-on sentence** is two or more sentences written together as one, without correct punctuation or words like *and, but* and *or*:

> The moose stood quietly by the lake, he was huge!
> The wind blew, birds were chirping in the trees.

Make two sentences or combine them using words like *and, but,* and *or*:

> The moose stood quietly by the lake. He was huge!
> The wind blew, and birds were chirping in the trees.

A Read each sentence. If it is a complete sentence, write *C* in the blank. If it is a fragment, write *F* in the blank. If it is a run-on sentence, write *R* in the blank.

_____ 1. A full-grown male moose is called a bull.

_____ 2. Are called cows and calves.

_____ 3. Can be found in many of the world's forests.

_____ 4. Moose eat both land and water plants.

_____ 5. The moose has four stomachs, they help it digest its food.

_____ 6. Looking for bears and wolves, their main enemies.

_____ 7. Even a pack of hungry wolves cannot kill a full-grown moose.

_____ 8. Unless the moose is old, weak, or sick.

_____ 9. Moose have long legs, they can step over things three feet high.

_____ 10. This amazing animal eats 20,000 leaves a day, that's a lot of leaves!

B **Rewrite each sentence fragment as a complete sentence.**

1. Reindeer, also called caribou.

   _____

2. Are smaller relatives of the moose

   _____

3. Long journeys called migrations in spring and fall.

   _____

C **Rewrite each run-on sentence as two complete sentences.**

1. In North America, this animal is called the caribou, in Europe and Asia it is known as the reindeer. _____

   _____

2. In warmer weather, females lose their antlers, they give birth to calves.

   _____

3. Male reindeer have larger antlers than females, the males lose their antlers in the fall. _____

   _____

D **Rewrite each run-on sentence as one complete sentence by adding *or*, *and*, or *but*.**

1. In summer, food is plentiful, reindeer eat leaves, berries, grass, and mushrooms. _____

   _____

2. Food is hard to find in winter, reindeer paw at the snow to find food.

   _____

3. Reindeer eat lichen from the ground, they eat it from tree branches, too.

   _____

   _____

LESSON

12

OUR
CHANGING
ENVIRONMENT

Punctuating Dates and Places

 The different parts of a date are separated by commas:

December 3, 1951   May 19, 1567   Sunday, January 11, 2004

When a date appears in a sentence, there should be a comma after the year:

Dad was born on September 4, 1976, in Chicago.

A comma should separate the city and state in an address:

Muncie, Indiana   Montgomery, Alabama   Buffalo, New York

Follow the same rule for foreign cities and countries:

Rome, Italy   Tokyo, Japan   Cairo, Egypt

When a place name appears in a sentence, there should be a comma after
the state or country:

Dana's family is moving to Anoka, Minnesota, in the fall.

That movie was filmed in Paris, France, and Dublin, Ireland.

A **Read the sentences. Add the correct punctuation to each sentence.**

1. A large oil spill took place near Anchorage Alaska on March 24 1989.

2. On March 16 1978 another large spill occurred near Portsall France.

3. A large oil tanker crashed on March 18 1967 near Land's End England.

4. Another oil spill, near Cape Town South Africa on August 6 1983 was caused by
   a fire on board.

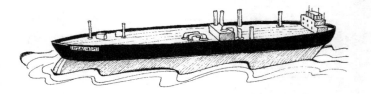

    Advantage Grammar Grade 3 © 2005 Creative Teaching Press

B Read the sentences. If the sentence is correct as written, write *Correct* on the line. If the sentence is incorrect, rewrite it correctly on the lines.

1. Jacques Cousteau, the famous ocean explorer, was born on June 11, 1910, in Saint-André-de-Cubzac France. _____

_____

2. Cousteau's ship, the *Calypso*, anchored in 7,500 meters of water on July 29 1956. _____

_____

3. The *Calypso* sank on January 11, 1996, in Singapore harbor.

_____

_____

4. On June, 25 1997, Jacques Cousteau died.

_____

_____

C Write a paragraph about the birthdates and birthplaces of your family and friends. Use correct punctuation in all dates and place names.

_____

_____

_____

_____

_____

_____

_____

_____

_____

Name _____

Spelling Compound Words

⭐ A **compound word** is a single word made up of two or more words joined together. Many common compound words are spelled as one word:

blackbird   airplane   textbook   underwater

There are few rules on how to spell compound words. Study the examples above. Then spell other compound words that are similar to these in the same way.

A **Underline the compound word in each sentence.**

1. Pines, firs, and spruces are all evergreen trees.

2. Dozens of butterflies were perched on the branch.

3. It seemed like they were everywhere!

4. Mom set up a bird feeder in the backyard.

5. We saw a bluebird at our feeder this morning.

6. One afternoon last week, I saw a cardinal.

7. My homework assignment was to draw a bird.

8. From the bedroom window, I saw a squirrel's nest.

9. Let's go downstairs and tell Darnell.

10. Darnell was outside planting some flowers.

B **Each sentence contains a compound word. If the sentence is correct, write**
Correct **on the lines. If it is incorrect, rewrite the sentence correctly on the lines.**

1. Francis used a rowboat to collect water samples from the pond.

_____

_____

2. He had a harder time rowing upstream. _____

_____

3. It's fun to walk bare foot on the beach and look for shells.

_____

_____

4. Most of an iceberg is under the surface of the water. _____

_____

5. Hugo's grand mother is a scientist at the university. _____

_____

6. Is there a stranger animal than the anteater? _____

_____

7. Snakes huddle together in under ground dens to keep warm.

_____

_____

8. Ayisha loves every thing about science. _____

_____

9. The panda exhibit is right through that doorway. _____

_____

10. Because Wes's hand writing is good, he can take notes about our

experiment. _____

_____

Name _____

Spelling Words with *qu-*

⭐ Many English words are spelled with the *qu* combination. It is pronounced like *kw*. The *q* is always followed by *u* and another vowel.

quick   **qu**art   earth**qu**ake   **qu**ilt

Ⓐ **Complete each sentence with a word that is spelled with a *qu* combination.**

1. The leader of a bee hive is called the _____ .

2. The fresh snow covered the ground like a _____ on a cozy bed.

3. The terrible _____ knocked down buildings all over the city.

4. The forest was very _____ after the birds stopped their loud singing.

5. The porcupine's back is covered with sharp _____ for protection.

6. A goose honks, but a duck makes a _____ .

7. The two crows made so much noise I though they were having a nasty _____ .

8. The old stone _____ has filled in with water and makes a nice lake.

9. Nina asked a _____ at the meeting about the new bicycle path.

10. A fox has to be very _____ to catch a rabbit!

11. Four _____ make up a gallon.

12. Ice is solid, but water is a _____ .

13. Bob White is another name for the bird called a _____ .

14. How does an animal _____ to be an endangered species?

15. There are four _____ in a dollar.

B **Write as many other words as you can that contain a *qu*. The letters can come at the beginning or the middle of the word. Then show your *qu* words to a partner. Check the spelling of any words you are unsure of.**

_____

_____

_____

_____

_____

_____

_____

_____

_____

_____

_____

_____

_____

_____

_____

_____

15

OUR
CHANGING
ENVIRONMENT

Editing Your Work

 Editing your work is an important step in the writing process. Many tests ask you to show what you know about editing.

A **Jaime wrote an essay about grasslands. Help him revise and edit his work. Read Jaime's essay and follow the directions.**

Grasslands of the World

1) The world's grasslands are among its most important regions. 2) Grasslands are habitats for many different animals and plants. 3) A habitat is the place where a living thing is normally found. 4) Large grasslands can be found in North America, Asia, and South America. 5) Some of the best-known grasslands are the savannas of southern Africa.

6) The savanna is home to many large animals, it is home to smaller ones, too. 7) These include elephantes, giraffes, lions, ostrichs, rhinoceroses, and hyenas. 8) What is the reason for this? 9) The main reason is that the savanna has many different plants. 10) The different animals of the savanna eat different plants 11) They share the available food. 12) Some animals eat grass, while others eat leaves. 13) Some eat young grasses, while others eat taller grasses. 14) Of course, animals like the lion don't even eat plants. 15) Eat plant-eating animals! 16) The variety of food sources allows many different animals to live in the savanna.

1. Two plural nouns are misspelled in sentence 7. What are the correct spellings?

_____

2. What mistake does sentence 6 contain? How would you correct it?

_____

_____

3. What compound word occurs several times in the essay? _____

4. What mistake does sentence 15 contains? How would you correct it?

_____

Name _____

B Continue reading and editing Jaime's essay.

1) What makes a grassland a grassland? 2) This is an interesting kwestion. 3) Grasslands around the world have some things in common. 4) They have few trees. 5) In most grasslands, the change in temperature between summer and winter is great. 6) Another similarity concerns rainfall, there must be just the right amount. 7) The amount of rainfall must be low enough so that forests will not spread. 8) But there must be enough rainfall so that the grassland does not become a desert.

9) Most grassland grasses are perennials. 10) This means they grow year after year. 11) Some grasslands must catch fire every few years. 12) If the grassland is not burned, trees will creep into it. 13) Grasslands with farmes on them can be very fertile. 14) The great prairies of the midwestern United States.

1. Does sentence 5 contain any singular nouns? If so, write them on the line.

_____

2. What mistake does sentence 6 contain? How would you correct it?

_____

_____

3. A word is misspelled in sentence 13. Rewrite it correctly.

_____

4. What compound word occurs in sentence 6?

_____

5. A word is misspelled in sentence 2. Rewrite it correctly.

_____

6. What mistake does sentence 14 contain? How would you correct it?

_____

_____

Name _____

Take a Test Drive

Fill in the bubble beside the correct answer.

Melissa is preparing a class report on her favorite animal—the bat! Help her revise and edit her facts before she writes her report. Read the facts and answer the questions that follow.

1) Notes on Bats   **2) May, 12 2004**

3) Bats are nocturnal. 4) They hunt during the night and sleep during the day. 5) Many kinds of bats live in caves. 6) Inside caves, the temperature does not change very much. 7) Bats also like the high humidity deep inside caves. 8) Bats often hang upside down from cave ceilings, cling with the claws on their toes. 9) Some caves have been home to bat colonies for thousands of years.

1. How should the date in sentence 2 be written?
Ⓐ May 12 2004
Ⓑ May, 12, 2004
Ⓒ May 12, 2004
Ⓓ It is correct as written.

2. Which sentence contains a compound word?
Ⓕ sentence 4   Ⓗ sentence 8
Ⓖ sentence 5   Ⓙ sentence 9

3. Which statement is NOT true about sentence 4?
Ⓐ It is a run-on sentence.
Ⓑ It is a complete sentence.
Ⓒ It does not contain a compound word.
Ⓓ It is not a sentence fragment.

4. Sentence 8 needs to be corrected. How would you correct it?
Ⓕ Bats often hang upside down. From cave ceilings, cling with the claws on their toes
Ⓖ Bats often hang upside down from cave ceilings. They cling with the claws on their toes.
Ⓗ Bats often hang upside down. From cave ceilings. Cling with the claws on their toes.
Ⓙ Bats often hang. Upside down from cave ceilings, cling with the claws on their toes

Advantage Grammar Grade 3 © 2005 Creative Teaching Press

Continue reading and editing Melissa's facts.

1) The only mammals that can fly. 2) Bats navigate in the dark by using a kind of radar. 3) They make a high-pitched sound and listen for echoes from cave walls. 4) Bats have fur, not feathers. 5) A bat's wing is leathery skin stretched from its sides to its finger bones 6) Bats are not dangerous to humans. 7) They are kwite harmless and avoid people. 8) A famous bat cave in the United States is Carlsbad Caverns, near Carlsbad, New Mexico.

5. Sentence 1 needs to be corrected. How would you correct it?
   Ⓐ Bats, the only mammals that can fly.
   Ⓑ Only mammals can fly.
   Ⓒ Bats are the only mammals that can fly.
   Ⓓ The only mammals that can fly, bats.

6. Which statement is true about sentence 6?
   Ⓕ It has no plural nouns.
   Ⓖ It has no singular nouns.
   Ⓗ It is not a complete sentence.
   Ⓙ It is a fragment.

7. A word is misspelled in sentence 7. What is the correct spelling?
   Ⓐ quite
   Ⓑ harmles
   Ⓒ evoid
   Ⓓ poeple

8. How should the place name in sentence 8 be written?
   Ⓕ Carlsbad New Mexico.
   Ⓖ Carlsbad, New, Mexico.
   Ⓗ Carlsbad. New Mexico.
   Ⓙ It is correct as written.

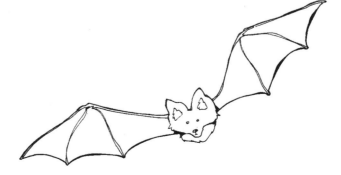

Name _____

Subject/Verb Agreement

⭐ Subjects and verbs must agree. Singular subjects must have singular verbs:

Our (planet) revolves around the sun.
(Pluto) is the smallest planet.
(I) am interested in the solar system

Plural subjects must have plural verbs:

The (planets) are very different.
(Venus and Mars) resemble Earth most closely.
(We) study the planets in class.

A **Look at the underlined verb in each sentence. Write _S_ on the line if the subject is singular or _P_ if the subject is plural. Then circle the subject of the sentence.**

1. Mercury and Venus <u>are</u> the closest planets to the sun. ___

2. Several planets <u>have</u> one or more moons. ___

3. Planet <u>comes</u> from the Greek word for "wanderer." ___

4. The moon <u>takes</u> 29-1/2 days to go around the Earth. ___

5. Moons <u>shine</u> because of reflected sunlight. ___

6. Scientists <u>study</u> the planets with telescopes. ___

7. A year on Venus <u>lasts</u> only 225 Earth days. ___

8. Mercury <u>gets</u> its name from the swift messenger of the Roman gods. ___

Advantage Grammar Grade 3 © 2005 Creative Teaching Press

B Circle the word that correctly completes the sentence.

1. The sun (are/is) at the center of our solar system.

2. The planets (moves/move) around the sun.

3. The planets and sun (is/are) not the only members of the solar system.

4. Icy balls called comets (zooms/zoom) through the solar system.

5. Asteroids (orbits/orbit) the sun in belts.

6. The largest belt (lies/lie) between Mars and Jupiter.

7. The largest asteroid (measures/measure) almost 500 miles across.

8. Dust particles in space, called meteoroids, usually (burns/burn) up before they reach Earth.

C Imagine you could take a spaceship ride to another planet. Write a paragraph about your ride and about your visit to the planet. Then exchange papers with a partner. Underline each subject and verb in your partner's paper. Then work with your partner to decide if each subject and verb is singular or plural.

_____

_____

_____

_____

_____

_____

_____

18

THE SOLAR SYSTEM

Writing with Correct Subjects and Verbs

⭐ Some special situations make correct subject-verb agreement more confusing. Be careful when a phrase comes between the subject and verb:

A **group** of students **looks** through the telescope.

The subject is *group*. It takes a singular verb. The word *students* is part of a phrase.

The **flowers** by the road **are** daisies.

The subject is *flowers*. It takes a plural verb. The word *road* is part of a phrase.

Don't be confused by questions. When the verb or part of the verb comes before the subject, they must still agree.

Is that your star chart?

The subject is *that*. It takes a singular verb.

Are Devin and Molly interested in the planets?

The subject is *Devin* and *Molly*. It takes a plural verb.

A Circle the word that correctly completes the sentence.

1. The planets in the solar system (is/are) all different.

2. (Does/Do) you have a favorite planet?

3. Meteoroids from space sometime (crash/crashes) into the earth.

4. Then they (is/are) called meteorites.

5. (Has/Have) she ever seen a large crater?

6. When (is/are) the trip to the space museum?

7. The girls in the back row (talks/talk) all the time.

8. What (is/are) a shooting star?

 Advantage Grammar Grade 3 © 2005 Creative Teaching Press

Name _____

B **Read each sentence. If the verb is correct, write *Correct* on the line. If the sentence is incorrect, rewrite the verb correctly on the line.**

1. The planet Venus is named after the Roman goddess of love. _____

2. Thick clouds on the planet reflects back light. _____

3. This cloud covering trap heat on Venus. _____

4. These clouds make Venus four time hotter than boiling water. _____

5. Another name for Venus are the morning or evening star. _____

6. You can, without a telescope, sees Venus for much of the year. _____

7. Life is not possible on Venus. _____

8. How does we know this? _____

9. The heat and carbon dioxide is the reasons. _____

10. Does people need oxygen to breathe? _____

C **What might your class see and do on a trip to a space museum? Write a paragraph describing a trip like this. After you finish, go back and underline each verb in your paragraph. Check to see that each verb agrees with its subject.**

_____

_____

_____

_____

_____

_____

_____

LESSON

19

THE SOLAR SYSTEM

Declarative Sentences

⭐ A **declarative sentence** makes a statement. It is followed by a period.

Jupiter is the largest planet.
However, it is smaller than the sun.
This planet has a famous red spot.
I think it's the most beautiful planet.

Think of a declarative sentence as the answer to a question. For example:

"What time is it?"
"It's 4 o'clock."

The answer to the question is a declarative sentence.

A **Read each sentence. Place a checkmark in the blank if the sentence is a declarative sentence.**

_____ **1.** Many of the planets have moons.

_____ **2.** Do you know which planet has the most moons?

_____ **3.** Take a guess.

_____ **4.** Jupiter has at least 16 moons.

_____ **5.** The two largest are called Ganymede and Callisto.

_____ **6.** Saturn has 18 moons.

_____ **7.** Have you ever seen Saturn's rings?

_____ **8.** Did you know that Jupiter is named after the king of the Roman gods?

_____ **9.** I wonder what the red spot on Jupiter really is.

_____**10.** Do scientists know?

_____ **11.** Most believe it is a storm on the planet's surface.

_____**12.** Think of that!

 Advantage Grammar Grade 3 © 2005 Creative Teaching Press

B Write a declarative sentence to answer each question.

1. What is his favorite planet? _____

_____

2. What is the name of the museum? _____

_____

3. Why would you like to be an astronaut? _____

_____

4. Why don't you want to be an astronaut? _____

_____

5. When did you visit Cape Kennedy Space Center? _____

_____

C Think about the sky at night. Write five declarative sentences about the night sky.

_____

_____

_____

_____

_____

_____

_____

_____

_____

_____

_____

_____

Interrogative Sentences

20

THE SOLAR
SYSTEM

 Another kind of sentence is the **interrogative sentence.** It asks a question. It is always followed by a question mark. In many interrogative sentences, part of the verb comes before the subject:

Is Sandra a good reader?   Does Ms. Wong teach science?
Did you wish on a star?   Can you name the planets?

Many other interrogative sentences use question words. Some common question words are *who, what, when, where, why, how, how many,* and *how much.*

When will the moon be full?   Where is the space ship?
What is a meteorite?   Who is the commander?
Why is Mars red?

A **Read each sentence. Place a checkmark in the blank if the sentence is an interrogative sentence. Then add a question mark at the end of the sentence.**

___ **1.** Which planet is the most like ours

___ **2.** Many scientists say that Mars is most like Earth

___ **3.** What is the size of Mars

___ **4.** Is it about half as big as the earth

___ **5.** How long is a day on Mars

___ **6.** Is it about as long as our day

___ **7.** Yes, it is

___ **8.** Mars also has changes in weather

___ **9.** Does it rain and snow on Mars

___ **10.** Go to the library and find out

Name _____

B Have you ever seen the TV show *Jeopardy?* People have to think up a question that goes with a given answer. Read these sentences. They are declarative sentences that make a statement. Write an interrogative sentence that the statement could be an answer to.

1. It is a large planet with rings. _____

_____

2. Mickey Mouse's dog was named after this tiny planet. _____

_____

3. They include the sun, planets, comets, asteroids, and meteorites. _____

_____

4. It has a long tail made up of dust and gas and flies through the solar system.

_____

5. They make huge craters when they strike the earth. _____

_____

C What would you like to know about space, the planets, and our solar system? Write five questions you would like to ask a space scientist or astronaut. Make sure your questions are complete interrogative sentences that end with question marks.

_____

_____

_____

_____

_____

_____

Name _____

L E S S O N

21

THE SOLAR SYSTEM

Spelling: Consonant Doubling

⭐ Many one-syllable words double their final consonant when *-ing* and *-ed* endings are added.

We plan to land on Mars.
We plan<u>n</u>ed to land on the moon.
We are plan<u>n</u>ing to explore space.

Follow this rule only when the final consonant has a single vowel in front of it. The final *n* in *plan* has the vowel *a* in front of it.

A **Look at each underlined word. If it is spelled correctly, write *C* on the line. If it is spelled incorrectly, rewrite it correctly on the line.**

1. Is Janelle <u>siting</u> in the driver's seat of the space ship? _____

2. Who <u>tapped</u> on the door of the cabin? _____

3. The spaceship <u>fliped</u> over in flight. _____

4. Do astronauts need to be good <u>swimers</u>? _____

5. I'm <u>getting</u> excited about the visit to the space museum! _____

6. The teacher <u>pluged</u> in the VCR. _____

7. Her subject of the video is "<u>Wining</u> the Race to Mars." _____

8. The pilot <u>sipped</u> his coffee before takeoff. _____

9. A NASA badge is <u>pined</u> to his spacesuit. _____

10. All the crew members <u>jogged</u> to stay in shape. _____

 Advantage Grammar Grade 3 © 2005 Creative Teaching Press

Name _____

 Do not double the final consonant if two vowels come before it:

> A rocket is faster than a speeding car.
> Did you see the astronaut eating her space food?

Do not double the final consonant if another consonant comes before it:

> People are camping on the beach to watch the blast-off.
> Dad talked on the phone to the guide.

B **Look at each underlined word. If it is spelled correctly, write C on the line. If it is spelled incorrectly, rewrite it correctly on the line.**

1. Professor Adams is <u>waitting</u> to give a speech. _____

2. She is <u>talkking</u> about the rings of Saturn. _____

3. People <u>coming</u> late will not be seated. _____

4. What are these names <u>listed</u> on the program? _____

5. The jet <u>dipped</u> its wings as it flew past. _____

6. The professor <u>sliped</u> out the side door of the auditorium. _____

C **Add the ending to the word and write the new word on the line. Double the consonant if necessary.**

1. spin + ing _____

2. bat + ed _____

3. gag + ed _____

4. feed + ing _____

5. stomp + ed _____

6. spit + ing _____

LESSON

22

THE SOLAR SYSTEM

Paragraph Structure and Style

⭐ A paragraph is a group of sentences about a single main idea, or topic. The main idea is usually introduced in a sentence called the **topic sentence**. The topic sentence often comes first.

> For centuries, people have looked in wonder at Jupiter's amazing red spot. Preparing and eating food in space is a special challenge. Does the red planet have water?

Other sentences in the paragraph include **supporting details**. For example, a paragraph about Jupiter's red spot might include:

- how big it is   • when it was first seen   • what it is made of

When writing a paragraph, indent the first sentence. This shows the reader that a new paragraph has begun. If you are writing on a computer, press the TAB key to indent the first sentence. Some writers prefer to skip a line between paragraphs and not indent. This is called **block style**.

 A **Read this paragraph. Then answer the questions.**

1) The discovery of Uranus in 1781 caused quite a stir! 2) Until then, scientists believed that Saturn was the last planet in the solar system. 3) A British scientist named William Herschel changed all that. 4) He looked through his homemade telescope. 5) Herschel saw a small object that looked green! 6) It turned out to be Uranus. 7) The new planet was twice as far from the sun as Saturn. 8) This means the known size of the solar system doubled!

1. Which sentence is the topic sentence?

    1   3   5   8

2. What is the purpose of sentences 2-8? _____

3. Is this paragraph in indented or block style? _____

Advantage Grammar Grade 3 © 2005 Creative Teaching Press

B **Plan and write a paragraph with a topic sentence and supporting details.**

Main idea: Exploring space is exciting.

Details to include:

_____

_____

_____

_____

My paragraph:

_____

_____

_____

_____

_____

_____

_____

_____

_____

_____

_____

_____

Name _____

Editing Your Work

 Editing your work is an important step in the writing process. Many tests ask you to show what you know about editing.

A Nat wrote an essay about life in the solar system. Help him revise and edit his work. Read Nat's essay and follow the directions.

Life on Other Planets

1) From earliest times, people have wondered if there could be life on other planets. 2) Books, movies, and TV programs shows aliens. 3) Sometimes, these aliens lookked like humans. 4) Other times, however, they were more like monsters. 5) What would life forms on other planets really look like?

6) Life forms on other planets would probably not look anything like people. 7) What is the reason for this? 8) Conditions on other planets are very different from Earth. 9) Therefore, the life forms that develop there would be very different too.

1. Which sentences are interrogative? _____

2. Is this essay in indented or block paragraph style? _____

3. Sentence 2 contains a mistake. How should it be rewritten correctly?

_____

_____

4. What is the main idea of the first paragraph? _____

_____

_____

5. What word is misspelled in sentence 3? _____

Advantage Grammar Grade 3 © 2005 Creative Teaching Press

B **Continue reading and editing Nat's essay.**

1) For example, no other planet has oxygen 2) Animals on earth needs oxygen to breathe. 3) Life forms on other planets would have to breathe something else. 4) Another problem is water. 5) Any water on other planets are probably frozen.

6) Most scientists do not believe that life exists on other planets in our solar system. 7) For a long time, people believved that there could be life on Mars. 8) Now we know that Mars is very cold and very dry. 9) Its atmosphere is too thin to breathe. 10) Terrible dust storms race across the planet's surface. 11) After a closer look, Mars does not seem like a good place for life!

1. What kind of sentence is sentence 1? Rewrite it with the correct end mark.

   _____

   _____

2. What mistake does sentence 2 contain? How would you correct it?

   _____

   _____

3. What mistake does sentence 5 contain? How would you correct it?

   _____

   _____

4. Write an interrogative sentence that could be the topic sentence of the first paragraph.

   _____

   _____

5. A word is misspelled in sentence 7. Rewrite it correctly. _____

6. Which sentence offers a detail to support the main idea of the last paragraph?
   Ⓐ sentence 8   Ⓒ sentence 10
   Ⓑ sentence 9   Ⓓ all of the above

7. Which sentence is the closing sentence of the last paragraph? _____

Name _____

Take a Test Drive

Fill in the bubble beside the correct answer.

Daniel's favorite planet is Pluto. So he was happy when he was assigned this subject for a class report. Help him revise and edit his report. Read the report and answer the questions that follow.

1) Until 1930, people thought there were only eight planets in the solar system. 2) Then, a man named Clyde Tombaugh gazzed into his telescope. 3) Way past Neptune, he saw a dark shape. 4) What could it be? 5) This was the smallest planet, Pluto!

6) Pluto is very hard to see, even with a telescope. 7) One reason is that it is dark all the time. 8) How did the planet gets its name? 9) Because it is so far away and so dark, it is nammed for the Roman god of the underworld.

1. Sentence 2 needs to be corrected. How would you correct it?
Ⓐ Then, a man named Clyde Tombaugh gazzed into his telescope?
Ⓑ Then, a man nammed Clyde Tombaugh gazzed into his telescope.
Ⓒ Then, a man named Clyde Tombaugh gazed into his telescope.
Ⓓ Then, a man named Clyde Tombaugh gazzed into his telescope?

2. Which statement is true about the first paragraph?
Ⓕ It contains an interrogative sentence.
Ⓖ It does not contain a declarative sentence.
Ⓗ It is not in indented style.
Ⓙ It contains a mistake in subject/verb agreement.

3. Sentence 8 needs to be corrected. How would you correct it?
Ⓐ How did the planet gets its name.
Ⓑ How did the planet get its name?
Ⓒ How didd the planet gets its name?
Ⓓ How did the planet gets its namme?

4. A word is misspelled in sentence 9. How should the sentence be corrected?
Ⓕ Because it is so far away and so dark, it is nammed four the Roman god of the underworld.
Ⓖ Becose it is so far away and so dark, it is nammed for the Roman god of the underworld.
Ⓗ Because it is so far away and so dark, it is named for the Roman god of the underworld.
Ⓙ Because it is so far awey and so dark, it is nammed for the Roman god of the underworld.

Name _____

Continue reading and editing Daniel's report.

1) Pluto is one of the most interesting planets. 2) It has a moon, Charon. 3) Charon is very close to Pluto. 4) It also has an odd orbit. 5) Sometimes, Pluto is actually closer to the sun than Neptune. 6) This is because Pluto's orbit is not round. 7) The planet gets inside Neptune's orbit! 8) Some scientists thinks this tiny ice ball is not a planet at all. 9) They think it might be one of Neptune's moons.

5. Which of the following sentences is a declarative sentence?
   Ⓐ sentence 2   Ⓒ sentence 8
   Ⓑ sentence 5   Ⓓ all of the above

6. Which statement is NOT true about sentence 5 ?
   Ⓕ It is a declarative sentence.
   Ⓖ It does not have a mistake in subject/verb agreement.
   Ⓗ Its subject is *Neptune*.
   Ⓙ It has no misspelled words.

7. Which sentence is the topic sentence of the last paragraph?
   Ⓐ sentence 1   Ⓒ sentence 7
   Ⓑ sentence 5   Ⓓ all of the above

8. Which statement is true about sentence 8?
   Ⓕ Its subject is *planet*.
   Ⓖ It has a mistake in subject/verb agreement.
   Ⓗ It is an interrogative sentence.
   Ⓙ It has a misspelled word.

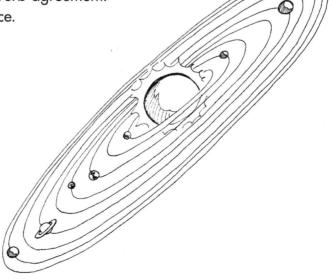

Name _____

25

HARRIET
TUBMAN

Identifying Pronouns

 Pronouns are words that replace or refer to nouns. The **personal pronouns** are *I, you, he, she, it, we, they, me, him, her, us,* and *them.*

> <u>I</u> read about Harriet Tubman in the book.
> Do <u>you</u> know about <u>her</u>?
> <u>She</u> helped many slaves escape to freedom.
> <u>They</u> followed <u>her</u> north.
> <u>It</u> is an exciting story.

Possessive pronouns show ownership. The **possessive pronouns** are *my, mine, your, yours, his, its, hers, our, ours, their,* and *theirs.*

> <u>Her</u> parents were slaves.
> <u>Their</u> lives were very hard.
> <u>Hers</u> was very hard, too.
> That book in <u>mine</u>.
> <u>Its</u> cover shows <u>my</u> hero, Harriet Tubman.

A **Underline the pronouns in each sentence.**

1. We do not know exactly when Harriet Tubman was born.

2. Her place of birth was eastern Maryland.

3. Harriet Tubman's family lived on their owner's farm.

4. They worked in the farm fields.

5. Its main crop was tobacco.

6. Hers was a life filled with back-breaking work.

7. Gazing at the North Star, she dreamed.

8. It pointed the way toward the North and freedom.

9. My heart aches when I read about Harriet Tubman.

10. Yours would too.

   Advantage Grammar Grade 3 © 2005 Creative Teaching Press

B Look at the underlined pronoun in each sentence. Write *Pers* on the line if it is a personal pronoun. Write *Poss* on the line if it is a possessive pronoun.

1. Have <u>you</u> ever heard about the Underground Railroad? _____

2. The Underground Railroad helped many slaves to *their* freedom. _____

3. <u>Our</u> class did a project on the Underground Railroad for History Day. _____

4. Ms. Logan asked <u>me</u> to read about Harriet Tubman. _____

5. Other classes prepared <u>their</u> projects for History Day. _____

6. <u>Theirs</u> were really good. _____

7. <u>I</u> won second prize. _____

8. The principal handed <u>me</u> a ribbon. _____

C Underline each pronoun in the paragraph.

Harriet liked to hear the older people tell stories. An old fellow seemed to know

a lot. She listened in wonder to his tales of life in the North. "Ours is a hard life," he

said. "But in the North, people are free, black and white. Children can go to school. No

masters, no whips." Little Harriet wanted so badly to believe him. *Their lives are so*

different from mine, she thought.

LESSON

26

HARRIET
TUBMAN

Using Pronouns in Writing

⭐ Pronouns are used to replace nouns in writing. In these sentences, the word *it* in the second sentence replaces *report* in the first sentence.

Leah gave a report on Harriet Tubman. It was really good.

In these sentences, the word *her* in the second sentence replaces *Leah* in the first sentence.

Leah's report was very interesting. I told her I really liked it.

Pronouns that replace nouns must agree with the nouns they replace. They must agree in **number** (singular or plural). They must also agree in **person** (first, second, or third). Finally, they must agree in **gender** (male, female, or neuter).

A Circle the word that correctly completes the sentence.

1. Harriet Tubman liked to sing a song. (Its/ Her) name was "Go Down, Moses."

2. The song told about Moses. (They/He) led the people of Israel out of slavery.

3. Moses' people were slaves in Egypt. (Them/They) were taken from Israel.

4. Harriet Tubman's people were also slaves. (My/Their) home was Africa.

5. Harriet's great-grandmother was stolen from Africa. (She/It) was taken to Baltimore.

6. Harriet had a friend named Old Cudjoe. She listened to (he/him) tell old tales.

7. Old Cudjoe was born on a slave ship. (Their/His) life began in slavery.

8. The last line of the song is "Let my people go." (They/It) had meaning for the slaves.

 Advantage Grammar Grade 3 © 2005 Creative Teaching Press

B Underline the pronoun in the second sentence. Then draw an arrow from it to the noun it stands for in the first sentence.

1. Cudjoe told Harriet about a special paper. It was called the Declaration of Independence.

2. The paper said all men were created equal. They all had rights.

3. Among the rights were life, liberty, and happiness. Slaves did not have them.

4. Harriet's heart grew sore. Her spirit was glum.

5. The slaves sang "Go Down, Moses." Would freedom ever be theirs?

C Write a sentence about a person you know. Then write another sentence that goes with it. Use a pronoun in your second sentence.

_____
_____
_____
_____
_____
_____

D Write a sentence about something you like. Then write another sentence that goes with it. Use a pronoun in your second sentence.

_____
_____
_____
_____
_____

Name _____

Using Pronouns in Writing

⭐ Some personal pronouns are used as the **subject** of a sentence. These include *I, you, he, she, it, we,* and *they*.

I read about the Underground Railroad.
Did you see the movie about Harriet Tubman?
She lived from about 1820 to 1913.
We visited her home on a trip to New York.
They sang "Go Down, Moses."

Other personal pronouns can never be used as subjects. Personal pronouns that cannot be used as subjects include *me, him, her, us,* and *them*.

A **Read each sentence. If it is correct, write C on the line. If the sentence is incorrect, rewrite it correctly.**

1. Him went to the meeting on Saturday.
   _____

2. Roy read the story to us.
   _____

3. After the play, us talked about the Underground Railroad.
   _____

4. Did they enjoy the play?
   _____

5. She played the part of Harriet Tubman.
   _____

6. Gary showed I the program.
   _____

7. Her goes to our school.
   _____

8. Them go to a different school.
   _____

9. We need to plan our History Day project.
   _____

10. Me can't think of anything right now.
    _____

B Write a complete sentence that answers each question. You can make up an answer, but it must make sense. Use one of the following pronouns in your answer: *I, you, he, she, it, we,* and *they*.

1. Where did Harriet Tubman live? _____
_____

2. What did the Underground Railroad do? _____
_____

3. What song did Harriet and her family sing? _____
_____

4. Who was Old Cudjoe? _____
_____

5. How do you and your classmates learn about history?
_____
_____

C Write sentences about people in history. Use the word at the beginning of each line in the sentence.

1. they _____
_____

2. her _____
_____

3. them _____
_____

4. him _____
_____

5. it _____
_____

Name _____

Capitalizing Geographical Names

⭐ The names of places should begin with capital letters. Places that should be capitalized include towns, cities, states, countries, continents, rivers, lakes, mountains, bays, and oceans.

Harriet Tubman was born in Maryland.
Slaves came from Africa.
They sailed on ships over the Atlantic Ocean.
The Underground Railroad crossed the Ohio River.
Many slaves escaped to Canada.

A **Read each sentence. If it is correct, write C on the line. If the sentence is incorrect, rewrite it correctly.**

1. One day, Harriet went to the town of bucktown. _____

_____

2. It was also in Maryland. _____

_____

3. She visited a Quaker at her Home. _____

_____

4. Quakers helped slaves escape to free parts of the Country. _____

_____

5. Harriet heard about another Quaker in the nearby state of Delaware. _____

_____

6. The Quaker told Harriet to follow the choptank River. _____

_____

7. The Choptank flows into Chesapeake Bay. _____

_____

8. "The Underground Railroad goes through camden," the woman said to

Harriet. _____

_____

Advantage Grammar Grade 3 © 2005 Creative Teaching Press

Name _____

B Follow the directions for each item. Be sure to use correct capitalization.

1. Write a sentence using the name of a country.

_____

2. Write a sentence using the name of a city.

_____

3. Write a sentence using the name of a river.

_____

4. Write a sentence using the name of a lake.

_____

5. Write a sentence using the name of an ocean.

_____

6. Write a sentence using the name of a state.

_____

C What country would you like to visit? Why? What would you like to see there? Write a paragraph describing the place you'd like to visit. Use correct capitalization for all place names.

_____

_____

_____

_____

_____

_____

_____

_____

Name _____

LESSON

29

HARRIET
TUBMAN

Changing from -y to -ies

⭐ Many words form their plurals by adding -s or -es. Other words add an s
to make the verb form that goes with he, she, or it.

There is a special spelling rule for adding endings to words that end in -y.
If the letter before y is a consonant, change the y to i and add –es:

lady—lad**ies**   carry—carr**ies**   library—librar**ies**

If the letter before the y is a vowel (a, e, i, o, or u), do not change the y
to i. Just add an s.

d**ay**—d**ays**   pl**ay**—pl**ays**   b**oy**—b**oys**

A **Look at each word. Add s, making any necessary spelling changes. Write the
new word on the line.**

1. carry _____

2. baby _____

3. marry _____

4. toy _____

5. factory _____

6. say _____

7. city _____

8. glory _____

9. joy _____

10. monkey _____

11. fairy _____

12. pay _____

13. dairy _____

14. enjoy _____

15. copy _____

16. valley _____

17. obey _____

18. story _____

19. turkey _____

20. stay _____

Advantage Grammar Grade 3 © 2005 Creative Teaching Press

B **Circle the word that correctly completes each sentence.**

1. The Underground Railroad often followed river (valleys/vallies).

2. Slaves escaping to the North stayed away from (citys/cities).

3. Enslaved (babys/babies) were sometimes separated from their parents.

4. It took many (days/daies) to reach the North.

5. Chesapeake Bay is one of America's largest (bays/baies).

6. (Ferrys/Ferries) took people across rivers and streams.

7. Enslaved (boys/boies) and girls began to work in the fields at an early age.

8. Harriet heard (blue jays/blue jaies) squawking in the trees.

9. Old Cudjoe told Harriet lots of interesting (storys/stories).

10. There were many different (ways/waies) to escape slavery.

C **Write a story about Harriet Tubman's life on the farm. Use as many of the words in the box as you can. If you need to add s, make the needed spelling changes to the word.**

| day play boy story baby city obey stay |
| say joy lady city carry |

_____

_____

_____

_____

_____

_____

_____

_____

Paragraph Structure

LESSON

30

HARRIET
TUBMAN

⭐ A paragraph is a group of sentences about a single main idea, or topic. Paragraphs can be organized in different ways. One way is **statement and example**. The paragraph makes a statement in the topic sentence. Then it gives examples that explain or support the statement.

Statement is in topic sentence.

Other sentences gives examples of how slaves had to be careful.

Escaping slaves had to be very careful on their journey to freedom. One mistake, and they could be caught. They had to walk through woods and forests. They could not use the roads. People might see them on the highways. Most traveled at night and hid during the day. Marshes and swamps were good hiding places. One great danger was dogs. A way to trick them was to walk in rivers and streams. That way, their keen noses could not find the trail!

A Write a paragraph about any subject you choose. Use statement and example organization. Begin with a statement as your topic sentence. Then give examples that support your statement.

_____

_____

_____

_____

_____

_____

_____

_____

_____

_____

_____

_____

Name _____

⭐ Another way to organize a paragraph is in **time sequence order**. This means you tell what happened first at the beginning. Then you tell what happened next, then next, and so on. Time sequence order works well for paragraphs that tell a story.

Topic sentence
tells what
happened first. ➝ Harriet decided tonight was the night she would escape. She went right back to her cabin after work. She collected a few things to take with her. She would need some food and her little bit of money. She also took a sharp

Other
sentences tell
what she did
and in what
order. ➝ knife. Would she have to use it? she wondered. Next, Harriet tied all the things up in a small bag. She took a final look around at her small cabin. Then Harriet walked out and closed the door quietly.

B Write a paragraph about any subject you choose. Use time sequence order organization. Begin with a topic sentence. Then tell what happened next, in time order.

_____
_____
_____
_____
_____
_____
_____
_____
_____
_____
_____
_____

LESSON

31

HARRIET
TUBMAN

Editing Your Work

 Editing your work is an important step in the writing process. Many tests ask you to show what you know about editing.

 A **Sunil wrote an essay about Harriet Tubman. Help him revise and edit his work. Read Sunil's essay and follow the directions.**

1) Harriet Tubman finally escaped from slavery in 1849. 2) She settled in philadelphia, Pennsylvania. 3) Pennsylvania was a free state. 4) It did not allow slavery.

5) Harriet found work and began to earn some money. 6) She washed clothes for fine ladys and gentlemen. 7) She also cooked food and cleaned houses.

8) However, one thing always ate at Harriet's heart. 9) Her own family, and other people's familys, still wore the chains of slavery. 10) Harriet had a more important job to do! 11) She became a conductor on the Underground Railroad.

1. Sentence 2 has a mistake. Rewrite it correctly on the lines. _____

_____

2. Look at sentence 4. The pronoun *It* refers to a word in sentence 3. What is the word? _____

3. Sentence 6 has a mistake. Rewrite it correctly on the lines.

_____

_____

4. What is the possessive pronoun in sentence 9? _____

5. Sentence 9 has a mistake. Rewrite it correctly on the lines.

_____

_____

6. What is the personal pronoun in the third paragraph? _____

 Advantage Grammar Grade 3 © 2005 Creative Teaching Press

Name _____

B Continue reading and editing Sunil's essay.

1) Harriet Tubman rescued she brother and some others in a daring rescue. 2) It was Christmas time, and freezing rain filled the skys. 3) The slaves left the farm. 4) The masters were singing Christmas carols in the house. 5) While they sang, Harriet led the slaves into the woods. 6) They were cold and freezing, but she did not let them have a fire.

7) Harriet Tubman walked up to a house. 8) A free black man lived there. 9) Harriet knew it was a stop on the Underground Railroad. 10) Her knocked the secret knock. 11) To her surprise, a white man leaned out a window. 12) Harriet asked for her friend. 13) The man snarled and said, "He was chased out of Town! Now, get away from my house!"

1. What kind of organization do these paragraphs use?

_____

2. Sentence 1 has a mistake. Rewrite it correctly on the lines.

_____

_____

3. Sentence 2 has a mistake. Rewrite it correctly on the lines.

_____

_____

4. Look at sentence 9. The pronoun *it* refers to a word in an earlier sentence. What is the word and what sentence is it in? _____

5. Sentence 10 has a mistake. Rewrite it correctly on the line.

_____

6. Sentence 13 has a mistake. Rewrite it correctly on the lines.

_____

_____

Name _____

Take a Test Drive

Fill in the bubble beside the correct answer.

Carmen is also writing a report about Harriet Tubman's adventures. Help her revise and edit the report. Read the report and answer the questions that follow.

   1) Over time, Harriet Tubman became famous. 2) She made dozens of trips to rescue slaves. 3) With each trip, her fame grew. 4) Slaves in the South had a special name for her. 5) They called her Moses. 6) Like Moses in the Bible, she was leading her people out of slavery. 7) Like Moses, she was taking them to the Promised Land.

   8) Slaves began to tell fantastic storys about Harriet. 9) *She was the tallest woman who ever lived*, some said. 10) Other claimed her eyes could see in the dark like a cat's. 11) *She climbs trees like a opossum and runs faster than a rabbit*, the children said.

1. Which statement is true about the first paragraph?
   Ⓐ It uses time sequence order organization.
   Ⓑ It uses statement and example organization.
   Ⓒ It contains no possessive pronouns.
   Ⓓ It contains no personal pronouns.

2. Which statement is true about sentence 5?
   Ⓕ The subject, *they*, refers to a noun in sentence 4.
   Ⓖ It contains a possessive pronoun.
   Ⓗ It has a capitalized place name.
   Ⓙ It has no personal pronouns.

3. Which statement is NOT true about the second paragraph?
   Ⓐ It uses time sequence order organization.
   Ⓑ It contains a personal pronoun.
   Ⓒ It does not contain a possessive pronoun.
   Ⓓ It does not use statement and example organization.

4. Which word in the second paragraph is misspelled?
   Ⓕ storeys   Ⓗ trees
   Ⓖ eyes   Ⓙ said

Name _____

Continue reading and editing Carmen's report.

1) The slave owners said other things about Harriet Tubman. 2) *We've got to stop her*, they said. 3) *She is stealing our property*. 4) Soon, there was a $40,000 reward for her capture—dead or alive! 5) But nothing stopped the fearless Harriet Tubman.

6) Her fame spread to many states and even other countrys. 7) A group in scotland sent money to help her work. 8) In the end, only one thing could stop Harriet Tubman. 9) What was it? 10) In 1861, the Civil War began. 11) Four years of war helped Harriet's dream come true. 12) In 1865, the war ended, and all the slaves were set free.

5. Which sentence contains a possessive pronoun?
   Ⓐ both sentences 3 and 4
   Ⓑ sentence 3
   Ⓒ sentence 2
   Ⓓ No sentence contains a possessive pronoun.

6. Which statement is true about sentence 6?
   Ⓕ It contains a mistake in capitalizing place names.
   Ⓖ It contains a spelling mistake.
   Ⓗ It contains a personal pronoun.
   Ⓙ It uses statement and example organization.

7. Which sentence contains a mistake in capitalizing the names of places?
   Ⓐ sentence 6
   Ⓑ sentence 7
   Ⓒ sentence 10
   Ⓓ sentence 11

8. Look at sentence 9. The word *it* refers to a word in an early sentence. Which one?
   Ⓕ fame in sentence 6
   Ⓖ money in sentence 7
   Ⓗ thing in sentence 8
   Ⓙ end in sentence 8

Name _____

Identifying Adjectives

 Adjectives describe nouns and pronouns. The underlined words are adjectives:

Americans love <u>tall</u> tales.

tall tells what kind of *tales* Americans love

There are stories about <u>different</u> heroes.

different describes what kind of *heroes* the stories are about

Paul Bunyan is <u>famous</u>.

famous tells something about *Paul Bunyan*

John Henry was <u>strong</u> as a mule.

strong describes *John Henry*

A **Underline the adjectives in each sentence. Draw an arrow from the adjective to the word it describes.**

1. Paul Bunyan was a huge baby.

2. He was born in the eastern state of Maine.

3. When the baby rolled around, he knocked over tall trees.

4. After he grew up, he decided the East was too small for him.

5. Paul moved to the large states of Wisconsin and Minnesota.

6. Paul became a logger and began cutting down gigantic trees.

7. Paul's favorite pet was an ox named Babe.

8. Babe was very gentle.

9. There was just one strange thing about Babe.

10. Babe was blue!

B **Underline each adjective in the paragraph.**

Babe was an amazing animal. If a road was too crooked for hauling logs, Babe could fix that. Paul just hooked him up to the road and Babe pulled until it was straight. Babe caused some big problems, though. If he was thirsty, he could drink a whole river. Then the logs couldn't float. When Babe needed new shoes, there wasn't anywhere for him to lie down. Paul had to clear all of the Dakota Territory to make room!

C **Fill in each blank with an adjective that fits the sentence.**

1. The tall tales about Paul Bunyan are _____ .

2. He may have been a _____ person.

3. Then people started to make up _____ stories about him.

4. Logging was a _____ job.

5. Babe was quite _____ .

6. He could pull _____ logs.

7. Paul and Babe wandered the _____ forests of Minnesota and Wisconsin.

8. Our class saw a _____ play about Paul Bunyan.

LESSON

MYTHS AND
LEGENDS

Using Adjectives in Writing

★ Adjectives answer these questions: *What kind? How many?* Numbers
are adjectives that answer the question *How many?*

The forest is beautiful. (answers the question What kind?)
We saw three woodpeckers. (answers the question How many?)

Adjectives often have end with *-ous, -y, -ful,* and *-ive.*

creepy   famous   beautiful   active

 A **Read each sentence. If it has an adjective, place a checkmark on the line and
circle the adjective.**

1. There were seven lumberjacks in Paul's crew. _____

2. They were hard workers. _____

3. Can you imagine how hungry they got? _____

4. The loved pancakes and biscuits. _____

5. The cook's pan was so big you couldn't see across it. _____

6. He had a special way to grease the pan. _____

7. Boys strapped hams to their shoes. _____

8. Then they skated across the gigantic pan! _____

9. Paul's biscuits were large as well. _____

10. He dropped one once and it caused an earthquake! _____

B Write a sentence of your own using each adjective.

1. scary _____

_____

2. orange _____

_____

3. dreamy _____

_____

4. quick _____

_____

5. boring _____

_____

C Write your own tall tale about Paul Bunyan. Use some of the adjectives in the word box.

| huge gigantic exciting dangerous funny silly powerful interesting |
| famous brave unknown modern heroic different great |
| important blue dark heavy light |

_____

_____

_____

_____

_____

_____

_____

Imperative Sentences

35

MYTHS AND LEGENDS

⭐ A **imperative sentence** makes a request or gives a command. It is usually followed by a period.

Shut the window, please.   Stay.   Get me some ice cream.

If the command is especially important or an emergency, it is followed by an exclamation point.

Don't touch that!   Stay out of the street! Look out, Danielle!

A **Read each sentence. Place a checkmark in the blank if the sentence is an imperative sentence.**

_____ **1.** Stop that, Babe.

_____ **2.** Don't pull on the rope.

_____ **3.** The logs are floating down the river.

_____ **4.** Some people say Paul Bunyan made the Great Lakes.

_____ **5.** Play the video.

_____ **6.** This video is about American tall tales.

_____ **7.** Don't forget the popcorn.

_____ **8.** Please tell me how to start the VCR.

_____ **9.** Turn on the power first.

_____ **10.** The tape is jammed.

_____ **11.** DVD players are better.

_____ **12.** Leave some popcorn for Brian.

 Advantage Grammar Grade 3 © 2005 Creative Teaching Press

Name _____

B Write an imperative sentence that answers the question.

1. What would you say to Paul Bunyan's cook if you were really hungry?

_____

2. What would you say to Babe if he was in your family's flower garden?

_____

_____

3. What would you say to Paul if you wanted him to chop you a Christmas tree?

_____

4. What would you say to Babe if he took off his ox shoes?

_____

5. What would you say if Paul Bunyan was walking around your neighborhood?

_____

6. What would you say if you were with Paul in the woods on a cold winter night? _____

_____

7. What would you say if you wanted Babe to sit down?

_____

_____

8. What would you say if you wanted a DVD from the library about Paul Bunyan? _____

_____

9. What would you say if you didn't want Paul to chop down all the trees in Dakota? _____

_____

10. What would you say if you were tired of hearing about Paul and Babe?

_____

_____

LESSON

36

MYTHS AND LEGENDS

Punctuating Titles of Books

⭐ The important words in **book title**s should begin with capital letters. Important words include nouns, verbs, and other longer words. Do not capitalize small words like *the, a, an, of, or, to,* and *and* unless they are the first word of the title.

American Tall Tales
All About Logging
The Adventures of Paul Bunyan and Babe
Folk Tales of the Great Lakes
The Road to Dakota
Paul Bunyan: Truth or Legend?

A Read each book title. If it is correct, write *C* on the line. If the title is incorrect, rewrite it correctly.

1. In Search of Paul and Babe _____

2. how to Be a Logger _____

3. The History of axes _____

4. Favorite songs of America's Lumberjacks _____

5. Life In The North Woods Of Canada _____

6. A Trip Across Lake Superior _____

7. A guide to Raising Oxen _____

8. 1000 Favorite Recipes For Pancakes _____

9. Ice Skating Made Easy _____

10. Born in Maine, raised in Minnesota _____

Advantage Grammar Grade 3 © 2005 Creative Teaching Press

B Make up a book title for the subject described. Be sure to use correct capitalization.

1. a book about how to put shoes on oxen

   _____

2. a book about how to dress like a lumberjack

   _____

3. a book about Minnesota

   _____

4. a book about buying a good axe

   _____

5. a book about identifying trees

   _____

6. a book about ships on the Great Lakes

   _____

C What good books have you read lately? Write an E-mail to a friend recommending some books you think he or she would like. Be sure to use correct capitalization when writing the book title.

_____

_____

_____

_____

_____

_____

_____

_____

_____

_____

Name _____

Spelling Common Homophones

⭐ Homophones are words that sound alike, but have different meanings. It's important to know which word you want to use and how to spell it. Here are 25 pairs that often cause trouble:

Ant is an insect. **Aunt** is your father's sister.

Bare is how trees look in the winter without leaves. **Bear** is a large animal.

Blue is a color. **Blew** is what the wind did yesterday.

Buy is what you do at a store. **By** means next to.

Cent is a part of a dollar. **Sent** is what you did to a letter yesterday.

Deer is an animal. **Dear** is how you begin a letter.

Dye means to color something, like cloth. **Die** means to stop being alive.

Eight is a number. **Ate** is what you did to lunch yesterday.

Guessed is what you did yesterday if you didn't know the answer.
     A **Guest** is someone who comes to your home

Hear is what ears do. **Here** is the opposite of there.

Hour is 60 minutes. **Our** means yours and mine.

Know means you understand something. **No** is they opposite of yes.

Male is the opposite of female. **Mail** is what the letter carrier brings.

Meet is when you run into someone. **Meat** is a food from animals.

New is the opposite of old. **Knew** means know, only in the past.

Pair means two of something. **Pear** is a fruit.

Red is a color. **Read** is what you did to a book yesterday.

Sale is where you can buy things. **Sail** is a piece of cloth that helps a boat go.

See is what eyes do. **Sea** is a large body of water.

Tale is a story. **Tail** is on the end of an animal.

There is the opposite of here. **Their** means something that belong to them.

Waist is the part of your body where you wear a belt. **Waste** means to not use something wisely.

Week means seven days. **Weak** is the opposite of strong.

Whole means all or everything. **Hole** is what you get when you dig in the ground.

Write is making letters and sentences. **Right** is the opposite of wrong.

Advantage Grammar Grade 3 © 2005 Creative Teaching Press

A If the sentence uses the underlined word correctly, write C on the line. If it is incorrect, cross out the wrong word and write the correct word on the line.

1. Bill needed the river as a <u>knew</u> source of water for his cattle. _____

2. He just started to dig a <u>whole</u> in the hard, dusty ground. _____

3. Pecos Bill could lasso a wildcat by its <u>tail</u>. _____

4. He could even lasso buzzards out of the sky <u>buy</u> their necks. _____

5. When he saw them up <u>their</u>, he just tossed his rope up. _____

6. I <u>here</u> he always let them go. _____

7. Like Paul Bunyan, Pecos Bill <u>ate</u> lots of biscuits. _____

8. It was an honor to be Bill's <u>guessed</u> at his ranch. _____

9. He would <u>meet</u> visitors, riding his horse. _____

10. Pecos Bill was the most famous man in the <u>hole</u> West. _____

B Write a sentence using each word.

1. cent _____

_____

2. deer _____

_____

3. dye _____

_____

4. mail _____

_____

5. write _____

_____

6. waste _____

_____

Name _____

Paragraph Structure

★ A paragraph is a group of sentences about a single main idea, or topic. Paragraphs can be organized in different ways. One way is **cause and effect.** In a cause and effect paragraph, either the cause or effect can come first.

Topic sentence tells the cause, or reason.

Other sentences tell what happened as a result of the cause.

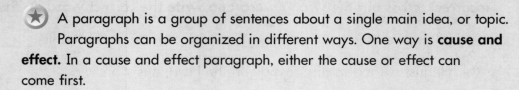

It rained and rained for more than a week. The creek on Bill's ranch got so high that it washed away its banks. Bill's cattle started to float down the creek. His chicken coop broke loose and was swept away by the rushing waters. When the water got up to Bill's front porch, he said, "I guess I'd better do something."

A Write a paragraph about any subject you choose. Use cause and effect organization. Begin with a topic sentence that describes a cause, or why something happened. Then tell the effects of the cause.

_____

_____

_____

_____

_____

_____

_____

_____

_____

_____

_____

_____

★ This paragraph first describes an effect, or the thing that happened. Then it gives causes, or reasons why the thing happened.

Topic sentence tells what happened.

Other sentences give reasons why it happened.

Pecos Bill became a favorite subject for cowboys all across the West. Why was this? The life of a cowboy could be lonely. Around evening campfires, cowboys liked to tell stories to pass the time. They could invent adventures for Pecos Bill like the ones they had. They could express pride in their way of life through the tales about Bill.

B Write a paragraph about any subject you choose. Use cause and effect organization. Begin with a topic sentence that describes something that happened. Then tell reasons why it happened.

_____

_____

_____

_____

_____

_____

_____

_____

_____

_____

_____

_____

_____

_____

_____

_____

_____

_____

LESSON

39

MYTHS AND
LEGENDS

Editing Your Work

Editing your work is an important step in the writing process. Many tests ask you to show what you know about editing.

A **LeBron wrote a class presentation about some of Pecos Bill's adventures. Help him revise and edit his work. Read LeBron's presentation and follow the directions.**

   1) Partners, listen to this tall tale of Pecos Bill. 2) Bill's horse was named Widow Maker. 3) He fed him barbed wire when he was young. 4) This made him tough, but ornery! 5) Lots of people tried to ride Widow Maker, but Bill was the only one who could stay on him. 6) What do you think happened when Bill's friend tried to ride Widow Maker?

   7) Bill tried to talk his friend out of trying to ride Widow Maker. 8) The friend jumped on the horse. 9) Widow Maker looked around at the man. 10) He saw it wasn't Bill. 11) So the horse started to jump and buck and run around. 12) The rider thought he was doing all write. 13) He was holding tight and staying on the horse.

1. List four adjectives LeBron used in the first paragraph.

   _____

2. LeBron wants to make sentence 6 imperative. Rewrite it as an imperative sentence.

   _____

   _____

3. LeBron decided he needs an adjective in sentence 7. Rewrite the sentence and add an adjective. _____

   _____

4. Sentence 12 has a mistake. Rewrite it correctly on the lines.

   _____

   _____

5. Which sentence is an imperative sentence? _____

Advantage Grammar Grade 3 © 2005 Creative Teaching Press

B Continue reading and editing LeBron's presentation.

1) After a while, Widow Maker decided he had had enough of this foolish rider. 2) Until now, the horse had only been messing around. 3) He bucked and kicked so hard the man flew right off. 4) He shot up into the clear blew sky. 5) Nobody knew where he had gone.

6) While Widow Maker munched some tasty green grass, Bill looked through his big telescope. 7) Where was that crazy rider? 8) Finally, Bill looked towards Pike's Peak in Colorado. 9) Their, on the very top, was the man.

10) *That crazy fool*, thought Bill. 11) *There's only one thing to do.* 12) Bill got his lasso and swung it around over his head. 13) Then he threw the rope all the way to the top of the mountain. 14) He gave a yank and pulled the man back down. 15) If Bill hadn't rescued him, he probably would have starved!

1. What kind of organization does the first paragraph use?

   _____

2. What does the topic sentence in the first paragraph tell the reader?

   _____

   _____

3. Sentence 4 has a mistake. Rewrite it correctly on the lines.

   _____

   _____

4. List four adjectives LeBron used in the second paragraph.

   _____

   _____

5. LeBron has decided to add an adjective to sentence 14. Rewrite the sentence and add an adjective he might use.

   _____

   _____

Name _____

Take a Test Drive

Fill in the bubble beside the correct answer.

LeBron's friend Caitlin also likes stories about the Old West. She is writing a book report for class. Help her revise and edit the report. Read the report and answer the questions that follow.

1) My report is on the book Stories And Spellbinders Of The Old West by Mr. Chisholm Trail. 2) This book retells legends, tall tails, and stories of the cowboys of the West. 3) Mr. Trail has worked as a cowboy himself. 4) He has first-hand knowledge of a cowboy's life.

5) I enjoyed this book for several reasons. 6) The writing style is clear, but exciting. 7) The stories he has chosen are funny, serious, scary, and suspenseful. 8) The characters are all interesting. 9) The settings of the stories are different. 10) But each one is described very well.

1. Sentence 1 contains a mistake. How should the sentence be correctly written?
- Ⓐ My report is on the book *Stories and spellbinders of the old west* by Mr. Chisholm Trail.
- Ⓑ My report is on the book *Stories and Spellbinders of the Old West* by Mr. Chisholm Trail.
- Ⓒ My report is on the book *Stories and Spellbinders of The Old West* by Mr. Chisholm Trail.
- Ⓓ My report is on the book *Stories And Spellbinders of the Old West* by Mr. Chisholm Trail.

2. Which statement is true about sentence 2?
- Ⓕ The word *tails* should be *tales*.
- Ⓖ It contains no adjectives.
- Ⓗ It is an imperative sentence.
- Ⓙ It uses cause and effect organization.

3. Which statement is true about sentence 5?
- Ⓐ It is an imperative sentence.
- Ⓑ It contains a mistake with homophones.
- Ⓒ It is a topic sentence that describes a cause.
- Ⓓ It is a topic sentence that describes an effect.

4. What are the adjectives in sentence 7?
- Ⓕ funny, serious
- Ⓖ funny, serious, scary
- Ⓗ funny, serious, scary, suspenseful
- Ⓙ There are no adjectives in the sentence.

Name _____

Continue reading and editing Carmen's report.

1) Of course, the book contains many great stories about Pecos Bill. 2) It also has stories about other cowboys. 3) You will find cowboy songs. 4) You will read about the Pony Express, famous outlaws, and noble sheriffs. 5) You'll learn about cattle drives, round-ups, and train robberies, along with many other things.

6) I truly believe this book is better than O.L.D. Paint's *Famous Stories of the Cowboys*. 7) Read this book if you want to learn a whole lot about the Old West. 8) I no you will enjoy it!

5. Which sentence contains no adjectives?
- (A) sentence 8
- (C) sentence 4
- (B) sentence 7
- (D) sentence 1

6. What correction is needed in sentence 6?
- (F) *Famous Stories of the Cowboys* should be *Famous Stories Of The Cowboys*.
- (G) *Famous Stories of the Cowboys* should be *Famous stories of the Cowboys*.
- (H) *Famous Stories of the Cowboys* should be *Famous Stories of The Cowboys*.
- (J) No corrections are needed.

7. Which sentence is an imperative sentence?
- (F) sentence 1
- (G) sentence 3
- (H) sentence 5
- (J) sentence 7

8. Which statement is true about sentence 8?
- (A) It is an imperative sentence.
- (G) The word *no* should be *know*.
- (H) It contains an adjective.
- (J) It is the topic sentence of the last paragraph.

Name _____

Using Compound Words

⭐ A **compound word** is a single word made up of two or more words joined together. Many common compound words are spelled as one word:

blackbird   bathroom   afternoon

Some compound words are nouns. They're used just like other nouns:

butterfly   backyard   airplane

Other compound words are adjectives. They are used just like other adjectives. Many compound adjectives are spelled with a hyphen:

underground   all-around   hard-to-read

A Underline the compound word in each sentence. On the line, write *N* if the compound word is a noun. Write *A* if it is an adjective.

_____ 1. I saw the Chinese New Year parade from the window in my bedroom.

_____ 2. Who own this good-looking Halloween mask?

_____ 3. The man in the dark-colored glasses is in the Christmas play.

_____ 4. There will be fireworks during the Fourth of July celebration.

_____ 5. Thanksgiving is an American celebration.

_____ 6. A Purim rattle is made of cardboard.

_____ 7. Our homework is to read about celebrations around the world.

_____ 8. Evergreen trees are decorated at Christmas.

_____ 9. In Mexico, people go to graveyards on the Day of the Dead.

_____ 10. My textbook tells abut Hina Matsuri, the Japanese doll festival.

B Write a sentence using each compound word.

1. downstairs _____

_____

2. candlelight _____

_____

3. sailboat _____

_____

4. everywhere _____

_____

5. dragonfly _____

_____

C Read each clue. Then write the answer on the line.

1. What is a compound word that means your mother's or father's father?

_____

2. What is a compound word that means knives, forks, and spoons?

_____

3. What is a compound word that means beneath the surface of a pond or lake?

_____

4. What is a compound word that means a large piece of frozen water floating in the ocean?

_____

5. What is a compound word that means walking without any shoes?

_____

Name _____

Exclamatory Sentences

 An exclamatory sentence expresses strong emotion. It is followed by an exclamation point.

Watch out!   That iron is hot!   Don't touch it!

Sometimes, an exclamatory sentence looks just like a declarative sentence. The way you can tell it expresses strong emotion is by the exclamation point.

Shut the door.   Shut the door!   Yes.   Yes!

 A **Read each sentence. Place a checkmark in the blank if the sentence could be an exclamatory sentence. Then add an exclamation point to the end of the sentence.**

1. Does your family celebrate Hanukkah _____

2. Children spin a special, four-sided top called a dreidl _____

3. You win _____

4. "Silent Night" is a famous Christmas carol. _____

5. I just love that song _____

6. The tradition of Christmas trees started in Germany. _____

7. Christians decorate Christmas trees. _____

8. You won't believe this _____

9. In Sri Lanka, some people decorate elephants _____

10. They are celebrating the Buddhist festival of Esala Perehera. _____

11. This celebration takes place each year in late summer. _____

12. There's a parade with dancers, acrobats, drummers, and even flame throwers

_____

Advantage Grammar Grade 3 © 2005 Creative Teaching Press

B Write a complete exclamatory sentence that answers each question. You can make up an answer, but it must make sense.

1. What would you say to warn someone about the burning candles on a birthday cake? _____

_____

2. What would you say when the Fourth of July parade is just about to start?

_____

_____

3. What would you say if someone scared you on Halloween?

_____

_____

4. What would you say if you ate too much Thanksgiving dinner?

_____

_____

5. What would you say on Memorial Day about school?

_____

_____

C Write a paragraph about how your family celebrates birthdays. At least one of your sentences should be an exclamatory sentence.

_____

_____

_____

_____

_____

_____

Name _____

LESSON

HOLIDAYS AND
CELEBRATIONS
AROUND THE
WORLD

Capitalizing Holidays

⭐ The names of holidays should always be capitalized.

Do you celebrate Ramadan?
Let's go to the Independence Day parade!
We eat turkey on Thanksgiving.
Holi is a spring festival for Hindus in India.
Is Kwanzaa the same time as Christmas?
Are you ready for Mother's Day?

A **Read each sentence. If it is correct, write C on the line. If the title is incorrect, rewrite it correctly.**

1. In what month do we celebrate Father's day? _____

    _____

2. In Brazil, a favorite holiday begins three days before Ash Wednesday.

    _____

    _____

3. It's the samba-dancing holiday known as carnival. _____

    _____

4. Japan celebrates a Holiday called Children's Day on May 5 each year.

    _____

    _____

5. Our holiday halloween comes from an ancient Celtic festival.

    _____

    _____

6. Jewish children dress up in costumes for purim, which takes place in late

    Winter. _____

    _____

B **Answer each question. Use correct capitalization when writing the name of a holiday.**

1. Write a sentence about a holiday that uses candles. _____

_____

2. Write a sentence about a holiday that is celebrated in the spring.

_____

_____

3. Write a sentence about a holiday when you have to get up early.

_____

_____

4. Write a sentence about a holiday that you don't celebrate, but a friend does.

_____

_____

5. Write a sentence about a holiday that honors your country.

_____

_____

C **Everyone has favorite holidays. What are yours? Write several sentences about how you celebrate your favorite holiday. Be sure to use correct capitalization when writing the names of holidays.**

_____

_____

_____

_____

_____

_____

LESSON

44

HOLIDAYS AND
CELEBRATIONS
AROUND THE
WORLD

Historical Periods, Special Events, and Days and Months

★ The important words in historical periods and special events should begin with capital letters. Important words include nouns, adjectives, and other longer words. Do not capitalize small words like *the, a, an, of, or, to,* and *and.*

the Revolutionary War   the Holocaust
the Twentieth Century   World War II

A Read each sentence. If it is correct, write C on the line. If the sentence is incorrect, rewrite it correctly.

1. In what year did the Revolutionary War begin? _____

   _____

2. It started in 1776 at the Battle Of Lexington. _____

   _____

3. It is also called the war of independence. _____

   _____

4. We read about the battle of Gettysburg. _____

   _____

5. It was the turning point of the Civil war. _____

   _____

6. That war took place in the nineteenth Century. _____

   _____

7. Dad's grandfather lived during the great depression. _____

   _____

8. That was before the Second World war. _____

   _____

     Advantage Grammar Grade 3 © 2005 Creative Teaching Press

Name _____

 The names of months and days are always capitalized.

>   February   April
>   Friday   Monday

B Write a word that correctly completes the sentence. Be sure to use correct capitalization when writing the name of a month or day of the week.

1. Easter is always on a _____ .

2. Another name for Independence Day is the Fourth of _____ .

3. My mom's birthday is _____ .

4. Our summer vacation starts in _____ .

5. Thanksgiving is the fourth _____ in November.

6. Easter can occur in March or _____ .

7. In the United States, elections are usually held on a _____ .

8. Will Passover start on a _____ this year?

9. Halloween is the last day of _____ .

10. My favorite day of the week is _____ .

Paragraph Structure

LESSON

45

HOLIDAYS AND
CELEBRATIONS
AROUND THE
WORLD

⭐ A paragraph is a group of sentences about a single main idea, or topic. Paragraphs can be organized in different ways. One way is **compare and contrast**. Compare means to tell how two or more things are the same. Contrast means to tell how they are different. Certain words give you a clue that a paragraph is comparing and contrasting. Some of these words are *and, both, on the other hand, however,* and *but.*

Topic sentence tells the main idea of the paragraph.

Other sentences tell how Mother's Days in England and France are the same and how they are different.

Both the English and the French celebrate Mother's Day. In England, the holiday falls on the fourth Sunday in Lent. In France, however, it is the last Sunday in May. Children in both countries like to fix breakfast for their mothers. Flowers are popular gifts. In England, daffodils are popular. On the other hand, French children often give their mothers roses.

A Write a paragraph that compares and contrasts how you celebrate Mother's Day and Father's Day in your family.

_____

_____

_____

_____

_____

_____

_____

_____

_____

Advantage Grammar Grade 3 © 2005 Creative Teaching Press

Name _____

★ Some paragraphs only compare two things. They tell only how they are the same. Other paragraphs only contrast two things. They tell only how they are different.

B Write a paragraph that compares two different holidays that you celebrate. Use words like *and* and *both*.

_____

_____

_____

_____

_____

_____

_____

_____

_____

C Write a paragraph that contrasts two different holidays that you celebrate. Use phrases or words like *on the other hand, however,* and *but.*

_____

_____

_____

_____

_____

_____

_____

_____

Name _____

Arranging Words in Alphabetical Order

⭐ Understanding **alphabetical order** is a very useful skill. Words in dictionaries and entries in encyclopedias are in alphabetical order. So are telephone books, class rosters, indexes, and many other things.

To place words in alphabetical order, start with the first letter. B comes before P, so

birthday comes before present

If the first letter of two words is the same, look at the second letter. A comes before R, so

party comes before present

If the first two letters of two words are the same, look at the third letter. A comes before E, so

pray comes before present

A Look at the words in each list. If they are in alphabetical order, place a checkmark on the line. If they are not in alphabetical order, draw an arrow from the word that is out of order to its correct place.

1. ___

Halloween
costume
mask

2. ___

Fourth
firecracker
parade

3. ___

pumpkin
table
turkey

4. ___

fabulous
father
mother
morning

5. ___

new
noisemaker
popcorn
party

6. ___

flowers
grave
memorial
soldier

B Look at the words in the list. Write them in alphabetical order on the lines.

parade   _____

celebrate   _____

flag   _____

family   _____

gift   _____

noise   _____

card   _____

flowers   _____

cookies   _____

rose   _____

light   _____

candy   _____

remember   _____

pumpkin   _____

give   _____

trick   _____

treat   _____

pie   _____

colorful   _____

firecracker   _____

C In the left-hand column, write 10 words about your favorite holiday or celebration. In the right-hand column, place your words in alphabetical order.

_____   _____

_____   _____

_____   _____

_____   _____

_____   _____

_____   _____

_____   _____

_____   _____

_____   _____

_____   _____

Name _____

47

HOLIDAYS AND
CELEBRATIONS
AROUND THE
WORLD

Editing Your Work

 Editing your work is an important step in the writing process. Many tests ask you to show what you know about editing.

 Kristin's family is Swedish-American. She wrote a class presentation about a Swedish holiday. Help her revise and edit her work. Read Kristin's presentation and follow the directions.

1) The holiday I'm reporting on is called the Saint Lucia Festival. 2) It takes place on december 13, one of the longest, darkest nights in Sweden. 3) This festival honors Saint Lucia. 4) She is the saint of light. 5) Every year, Swedish school children put on a special play and parade that honors Saint Lucia.

6) One student is elected to be Saint Lucia. 7) Other students are her attendants. 8) Saint Lucia leads the parade. 9) She is dressed in a white robe with a bright red sash. 10) Lucia also wears a crown made of evergreen leaves. 11) These leaves represent new life in the middle of the deep, dark Swedish winter. 12) On her crown are candles. 13) Sometimes the candles are real. 14) Other times they are electric. 15) The parade is beautiful in candlelight.

1. List three compound words Kristin used in the second paragraph.

   _____

2. Which sentence contains the name of a holiday? _____

3. What two things are contrasted in the second paragraph?

   _____

   _____

4. Sentence 2 has a mistake. Rewrite it correctly on the lines.

   _____

   _____

5. Write these words from Kristin's report in alphabetical order: *holiday, longest, honors, school, elected, white, red, crown, middle,* and *real.*

   _____

   _____

    Advantage Grammar Grade 3 © 2005 Creative Teaching Press

B Continue reading and editing Kristin's presentation.

1) The students sing a beautiful song about Saint Lucia. 2) Then they tell the story of the saint. 3) Often, students and their parents gather to eat special foods and sing more songs. 4) The best-known food for Saint Lucia are buns. 5) These buns are called Lucia cats. 6) They are made with a very expensive spice, saffron, and raisins. 7) The saffron turns the buns yellow. 8) Another favorite treat is extra-thin ginger snaps. 9) My dad can make them. 10) Boy, are they good!

11) Swedes love the Saint Lucia festival. 12) It comes 12 days before Christmas and helps start the Holiday season. 13) The festival also gives them hope. 14) Saint Lucia reminds them that the warm, sunny days of summer are not too far away!

1. Which two sentences are exclamatory sentences?

   _____

2. Which two sentences contain a compound word used as an adjective? What are the words?

   _____

3. Sentence 12 has a mistake. Rewrite it correctly on the lines.

   _____

   _____

4. If Kristin wanted to make the first paragraph a compare and contrast paragraph, what two things could she compare?

   _____

   _____

5. Write these words from Kristin's report in alphabetical order: *sing, song, story, saint, special, spice, saffron, snaps, season,* and *summer*.

   _____

   _____

   _____

Name _____

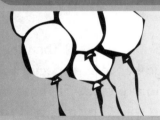

Take a Test Drive

Fill in the bubble beside the correct answer.

Kristin's friend Ahmed has also written a report. He is reporting on a Muslim holiday.

1) Muslims have a special way of celebrating the month of Ramadan. 2) We fast, or don't eat between sunrise and sunset. 3) Ramadan is a thoughtful time. 4) We think about God, or Allah, and remember poor and unhappy people. 5) Ramadan is our ninth month. 6) It ends the morning after we see the new moon in the sky.

7) The festival that celebrates the end of Ramadan is called Eid ul-Fitr. 8) Believe it our not, it actually means "breakfast"! 9) We call it this because we are "breaking our fast," the month of fasting for Ramadan. 10) Eid lasts three days, and this year it begins in september. 11) We begin the holiday by taking a bath and putting on new clothes. 12) Then we go to our mosque, before the sun is even up. 13) We say prayers until the sun has risen. 14) After mosque, we go home. 15) Then we get to eat whatever we want!

1. Sentence 10 contains a mistake. How should the sentence be correctly written?
   - Ⓐ Eid lasts three days, and this Year it begins in September.
   - Ⓑ Eid lasts three Days, and this year it begins in september.
   - Ⓒ Eid lasts three days, and this year it begins in September.
   - Ⓓ Eid lasts three Days, and this year it begins in September.

2. Which statement is true about the second paragraph?
   - Ⓕ It contains two exclamatory sentences.
   - Ⓖ It contains one exclamatory sentence.
   - Ⓗ It correctly capitalizes a historical period.
   - Ⓙ it uses compare and contrast organization.

3. What are two compound words in the second paragraph?
   - Ⓐ festival and breakfast
   - Ⓑ begin and celebrate
   - Ⓒ breakfast and whatever
   - Ⓓ There are no compound words.

4. Which statement contrasts Ramadan and Eid?
   - Ⓕ Both Ramadan and Eid are celebrated by Muslims.
   - Ⓖ Ramadan and Eid both mean "breaking the fast."
   - Ⓗ Muslims do not eat during either Ramadan or Eid.
   - Ⓙ Ramadan is for fasting, while Eid is for eating and celebrating.

Continue reading and editing Ahmed's report.

1) We have lots of special customs for Eid. 2) Like Christians do at christmas, we also send cards at Eid. 3) My relatives give me presents and money. 4) I put all the money I get in a special moneybox. 5) We have meals, with lots of family and friends. 6) Sometimes, we even invite poor people to eat with us. 7) People are always stopping by to visit during Eid. 8) We make sure we have candy and cookies to give them.

9) Because my parents are from Jordan, our Eid foods are mostly Jordanian! 10) I love Eid cookies called *ma'moul.* 11) They are made of flour, dates, and nuts. 12) My mom presses them with a special cookie mold.

5. Sentence 9 contains a mistake. How should the sentence be correctly written?
   - Ⓐ Because my Parents are from Jordan, our Eid foods are mostly Jordanian!
   - Ⓑ Because my parents are from Jordan, our Eid foods are mostly Jordanian.
   - Ⓒ Because my parents are from Jordan, our eid foods are mostly Jordanian!
   - Ⓓ Because my parents are from Jordan, our Eid foods are mostly Jordanian?

6. Which sentence contains a mistake in capitalization?
   - Ⓕ sentence 2
   - Ⓖ sentence 9
   - Ⓗ sentence 10
   - Ⓙ sentence 13

7. Which sentence makes a comparison?
   - Ⓐ sentence 2
   - Ⓑ sentence 6
   - Ⓒ sentence 7
   - Ⓓ sentence 11

8. Which choice arranges the words from Ahmed's report in alphabetical order?
   - Ⓕ make, money, meals, mold
   - Ⓖ meals, mold, make, money
   - Ⓗ mold, make, money, meals
   - Ⓙ make, meals, mold, money

Name _____

Read the paragraph and answer the questions.

   1) Each August, a wonderful festival takes place on the island of Sri Lanka. 2) It is the Buddhist holiday of esala perehera. 3) This holiday honors the Buddha, the founder of Buddhism. 4) The festival lasts 10 days and nights. 5) Elephants walk in the magnificent parade. 6) They wear beautiful costumes, decorated with tiny lights. 7) Dancers, drummers, and flame throwers. 8) Wouldn't you like to see the festival?

1. Sentence 2 contains a mistake. How should it be written correctly?

   Ⓐ It is the Buddhist Holiday of esala perehera.
   Ⓑ It is the Buddhist holiday of Esala Perehera.
   Ⓒ It is the Buddhist holiday of esala Perehera.
   Ⓓ It is the Buddhist holiday of Esala perehera.

2. Which word is an adjective in sentence 5?

   Ⓕ Elephants   Ⓗ magnificent
   Ⓖ walk   Ⓙ parade

3. Which statement is true about sentence 8?
   Ⓐ It is an interrogative sentence.
   Ⓑ It is a declarative sentence.
   Ⓒ It is a imperative sentence.
   Ⓓ It is an exclamatory sentence.

4. What is the main idea of this paragraph?
   Ⓕ This festival lasts 10 days and nights.
   Ⓖ Elephants in the parade wear costumes.
   Ⓗ This Buddhist holiday is wonderful.
   Ⓙ The festival takes place in August.

5. Sentence 7 needs to be corrected. Why?
   Ⓐ It is not a complete sentence; it is missing a pronoun.
   Ⓑ It is not a complete sentence; it is missing a verb.
   Ⓒ It is not a complete sentence; it is missing a subject.
   Ⓓ It is not a complete sentence; it is missing an adjective.

6. Which sentence contains a compound word?
   Ⓕ sentence 2   Ⓗ sentence 6
   Ⓖ sentence 5   Ⓙ There are no compound words in the paragraph.

Advantage Grammar Grade 4 © 2005 Creative Teaching Press

Name _____

7. Sentence 2 contains a mistake. How should it be written correctly?

Ⓐ I wish those babies would stop crying.

Ⓒ Who plays the king in that movie?

Ⓒ After I dig the hole, Dad carrys away the dirt.

Ⓓ Ohio has lots of big cities.

8. Which sentence uses correct punctuation?

Ⓔ Grandma was born April 24, 1942 in Boise Idaho.

Ⓕ Her family moved to Seattle, Washington, on June 15, 1946.

Ⓖ She married Grandpa on December, 10, 1965 in Portland, Oregon.

Ⓗ Dad, their first child, was born on August 18 1969, in Helena, Montana.

9. Which statement uses a correct plural noun?

Ⓐ The leafs are starting to turn color.

Ⓑ The days are getting shorter.

Ⓒ Bird are flying south for the winter.

Ⓓ There are many wayes to tell that fall is here.

10. Which sentence has correct end punctuation?

Ⓔ That's the worst joke I ever heard!

Ⓕ Where did you learn that one.

Ⓖ Don't tell me another one?

Ⓗ Did your sister tell you that one.

11. Which words are in alphabetical order?

Ⓐ Mars, Venus, Mercury, Saturn

Ⓑ Neptune, Pluto, moon, rocket

Ⓒ Jupiter, sun, solar, water

Ⓓ asteroids, comet, Earth, rings

12. In which sentence is the verb underlined?

Ⓔ Lewis and Clark left St. Louis <u>in</u> the spring.

Ⓕ The explorers <u>traveled</u> up the river.

Ⓖ Their boats were very <u>useful</u>.

Ⓗ <u>Everyone</u> suffered during the harsh winter.

Name _____

Practice Test

Read the paragraph and answer the questions.

1) Davy Crockett was born in eastern tennessee on August 17, 1786. 2) His family was poor, so Davy could not go to school. 3) He went to work right away. 4) He soon made his name as a rough frontiersman. 5) Davy ran for Congress in 1823, he served three terms. 6) Twelve years later, he decided to head to Texas. 7) There, he joined the defenders of the Alamo. 8) Davy Crockett died with them at the Battle Of The Alamo on March 6, 1836.

13. Which kind of organization does this paragraph use?

   Ⓐ Statement and Example   Ⓒ Cause and Effect

   Ⓑ Time Sequence Order   Ⓓ Compare/Contrast

14. Sentence 1 contains a mistake. How should it be written correctly?

   Ⓕ Davy Crockett was born in eastern tennessee on August, 17, 1786.

   Ⓖ Davy Crockett was born in eastern tennessee on August 17 1786.

   Ⓗ Davy Crockett was born in eastern Tennessee on August 17, 1786.

   Ⓙ Davy Crockett was born in Eastern Tennessee on August 17 1786.

15. Sentence 5 contains a mistake. How should it be written correctly?

   Ⓐ Davy ran for Congress in 1823, he served three terms!

   Ⓑ Davy ran for Congress in 1823. he served three terms.

   Ⓒ Davy ran for Congress in 1823, He served three terms.

   Ⓓ Davy ran for Congress in 1823. He served three terms.

16. Which sentence contains a compound word?

   Ⓕ sentence 1   Ⓗ sentence 3

   Ⓖ sentence 2   Ⓙ sentence 4

17. Sentence 8 contains a mistake. How should it be written correctly?

   Ⓐ Davy Crockett died with they at the Battle of the Alamo on March 6, 1836.

   Ⓑ Davy Crockett died with them at the Battle Of The Alamo on March 6, 1836!

   Ⓒ Davy Crockett died with them at the Battle of the Alamo on March 6, 1836.

   Ⓓ Davy Crockett died with them at the Battle Of The Alamo on March 6 1836.

18. Which sentences contain a possessive pronoun?

   Ⓕ sentences 2 and 4   Ⓗ sentences 6 and 8

   Ⓖ sentences 3 and 5   Ⓙ sentences 7 and 8

Advantage Grammar Grade 4 © 2005 Creative Teaching Press

19. Which sentence does NOT contain a mistake?

   Ⓐ You're going to love the natural history museum.
   Ⓑ I've never been their before!
   Ⓒ Its in a large building downtown.
   Ⓓ Did you remember you're permission slip?

20. Which sentence contains a spelling mistake

   Ⓕ If you are quick, you'll be able to see the rabbit.
   Ⓖ Please be kwiet at the back of the room.
   Ⓗ The guide made a telephone call.
   Ⓙ Which came first, the chicken or the egg?

21. Which sentence does NOT contain a spelling mistake?

   Ⓐ Desert plants often have thick leaves.
   Ⓑ Do you have any kwestions about the display?
   Ⓒ I think sppring is a beautiful season in the desert.
   Ⓓ A terrible earthqauke struck the area.

22. Which sentence contains a spelling mistake?

   Ⓕ Harriet Tubman is waiting in the forest.
   Ⓖ She talked about the Underground Railroad.
   Ⓗ The wheel on the wagon is spining around.
   Ⓙ Harriet knocked on the Quaker family's door.

23. Which book title uses correct capitalization?

   Ⓐ the Incredible Legend of Pecos Bill
   Ⓑ How to take Care of our Earth
   Ⓒ Traveling The Underground Railroad With Harriet Tubman
   Ⓓ Festivals and Celebrations Around the World

24. Which sentence is correct?

   Ⓕ Did you here that strange screech in the woods?
   Ⓖ Our camping trip lasted a whole weak.
   Ⓗ Tie this rope around your waste.
   Ⓙ Mom gave me a pair of hiking socks.

Lesson 1

A
1. Meriwether Lewis, William Clark, journey
2. Meriwether Lewis, friend, president
3. name, Thomas Jefferson
4. William Clark, soldier
5. St. Louis
6. trip
7. group, boat
8. Lewis, Clark, excitement

B
1. Indian
2. bear
3. desert
4. axe or saw
5. happiness

C

night, ear, fear, rest, east, courage, rag, wolf, star, eagle, forest, guide, noise, horse

Lesson 2

A
1. are
2. sits
3. is
4. studies
5. grow
6. blows
7. dream
8. recycles
9. flows
10. began
11. like
12. is

B
1. is
2. live
3. look
4. face
5. are

C (sample answers)
1. Pine trees grow tall in the mountains.
2. A small animal runs across the ground.
3. We camp in the national park.
4. The Rockies are in Colorado.
5. Hawks and eagles fly above the trees.

Lesson 3

A
1. Sacagawea was a Shoshone woman.
2. She helped Lewis and Clark.
3. The difficult journey lasted several years.
4. Lewis and Clark became heroes.
5. The two men received important government jobs.

B
1. President Thomas Jefferson bought a large amount of land.
2. In 1803, the United States bought the land.
3. The land belonged to France.
4. It included the important port of New Orleans.
5. Jefferson sent Lewis and Clark across the continent.

C
1. phrase
2. predicate
3. subject
4. phrase
5. predicate
6. subject
7. subject
8. phrase

Lesson 4

A
1. period
2. question mark
3. period
4. question mark
5. period
6. question mark
7. exclamation point
8. exclamation point
9. period
10. period

B
1. ?
2. correct
3. correct
4. .
5. correct
6. correct
7. .
8. . or !
9. .
10. correct

C
Sentences will vary but should correctly use each kind of end mark.

Lesson 5

A
1. ring
2. chick
3. push
4. throw
5. spring
6. splash
7. phone
8. beach
9. shed
10. long
11. cloth
12. child

B
Correct words are *spring, wing, shape,* and *both.*

C
Students' sentences should use and correctly spell the words *search, thick, hang, choose, thank, teach, bush,* and *shout.*

Advantage Grammar Grade 3 © 2005 Creative Teaching Press

Lesson 6

A
1. Isn't the Lewis and Clark story interesting?
2. In school, we're reading about their journey.
3. It's Megan's favorite part of U.S. history.
4. They're her two heroes!
5. I think she'd like to go to St. Louis.
6. She could've gone last summer.
7. Lewis and Clark couldn't speak with the Native Americans.
8. Without Sacajawea, they would've been in trouble.
9. You're giving a report today about the expedition.
10. I knew I wouldn't be there to hear it.

B
1. Is not?
2. we are
3. It is
4. They are
5. she would
6. could have
7. could not
8. would have
9. You are
10. would not

C
1. I'd
2. they're
3. you're
4. wouldn't
5. it's

D
Students post cards or E-mails will vary but should correctly use several of the common contractions listed in the lesson.

Lesson 7

A
1. Lewis, Clark, goals, journey
2. They wanted to discover a water route from the East to the Pacific Ocean.
3. you have; you've
4. the, sheep
5. made

B
1. in Idaho
2. share
3. sentence 10
4. 11 and 12 are incomplete; Last year, my uncle made the same trip.
5. Sentence 14; Here is.

Lesson 8
1. C
2. G
3. C
4. H
5. A
6. J
7. C
8. F

Lesson 9

A
1. Penguins live only south of the Equator.
2. Some, but not all, penguins live at the South Pole.
3. Many people enjoy learning about this interesting bird.
4. Penguins fit well into their environment.
5. Its coat of feathers is very dense.
6. They keep the penguin warm in cold weather.
7. Its wings work like flippers, moving the bird through the water.
8. The shape of its body also helps the bird swim.
9. One kind of penguin can swim 22 miles an hour!
10. The largest penguin can weigh almost 70 pounds.

B
1. place
2. thing
3. person
4. place
5. idea

C
Sentences will vary; students should correctly use and identify singular nouns.

Lesson 10

A
1. Many animals are cold-blooded.
2. Snakes, turtles, fish, and alligators are all cold-blooded.
3. These creatures take in heat from outside their bodies.
4. no plural nouns
5. That's why many of these animals hibernate, or sleep, during winter.
6. Many make nests in dry leaves, caves, or holes in the ground.
7. One of the largest cold-blooded animals is the komodo dragon.
8. Men and women who study animals are called zoologists.

B
1. knives
2. sheep
3. skies
4. hutches
5. reptiles
6. heroes
7. days
8. children
9. messes
10. potatoes

C
1. regions
2. ways
3. musk oxen
4. hooves
5. groups

Lesson 11

A
1. C
2. F
3. F
4. C
5. R
6. F
7. C
8. F
9. R
10. R

B
1. Reindeer are also called caribou.
2. Reindeer are smaller relatives of the moose.
3. They go on long journeys called migrations in spring and fall.

Answer Key

C

1. In North America, this animal is called the caribou. In Europe and Asia, it is known as the reindeer.
2. In warmer weather, females lose their antlers. They also give birth to calves.
3. Male reindeer have larger antlers than females. Males lose their antlers in the fall.

D

1. In summer, food is plentiful, and reindeer eat leaves, berries, grass, and mushrooms.
2. Food is hard to find in winter, but reindeer paw at the snow to find food.
3. Reindeer eat lichen from the ground or from tree branches.

Lesson 12
A

1. A large oil spill took place near Anchorage, Alaska, on March 24, 1989.
2. On March 16, 1978, another large spill occurred near Portsall, France.
3. A large oil tanker crashed on March 18, 1967, near Land's End, England.
4. Another oil spill, near Cape Town, South Africa, on August 6, 1983, was caused by a fire on board.

B

1. Jacques Cousteau, the famous ocean explorer, was born on June 11, 1910, in Saint-André-de-Cubzac, France.
2. Cousteau's ship, the *Calypso*, anchored in 7,500 meters of water on July 29, 1956.
3. correct
4. On June 25, 1997, Jacques Cousteau died.

C

Sentences will vary but should correctly punctuate all dates and places.

Lesson 13
A

1. Pines, firs, and spruces are all <u>evergreen</u> trees.
2. Dozens of <u>butterflies</u> were perched on the branch.
3. It seemed like they were <u>everywhere</u>!
4. Mom set up a bird feeder in the <u>backyard</u>.
5. We saw a <u>bluebird</u> at our feeder this morning.
6. One <u>afternoon</u> last week, I saw a cardinal.
7. My <u>homework</u> assignment was to draw a bird.
8. From the <u>bedroom</u> window, I saw a squirrel's nest.
9. Let's go <u>downstairs</u> and tell Darnell.
10. Darnell was <u>outside</u> planting some flowers.

B

1. correct
2. correct
3. It's fun to walk barefoot on the beach and look for shells.
4. correct
5. Hugo's grandmother is a scientist at the university.
6. correct

7. Snakes huddle together in underground dens to keep warm.
8. Ayisha loves everything about science.
9. correct
10. Because Wes's handwriting is good, he can take notes about our experiment.

Lesson 14
A

1. queen	9. question
2. quilt	10. quick
3. earthquake	11. quarts
4. quiet	12. liquid
5. quills	13. quail
6. quack	14. qualify
7. quarrel	15. quarters
8. quarry	

B

Students should list four or five words and spell them correctly, checking the spelling if necessary.

Lesson 15
A

1. elephants, ostriches
2. It contains a run-on sentence. Rewrite it as one sentence: *The savanna is home to many large and small animals.* or as two sentences: *The savanna is home to many large animals. It is home to smaller ones, too.*
3. grasslands
4. It contains a sentence fragment. Rewrite it with a subject and predicate: *The lions eat the plant-eating animals.*

B

1. temperature, summer, winter
2. It contains a run-on sentence. Rewrite it as two sentences: *Another similarity concerns rainfall. There must be just the right amount.*
3. farms
4. rainfall
5. question
6. It contains a sentence fragment. Rewrite it with a predicate: *The great prairies of the midwestern United States are one example.*

Lesson 16

1. C		5. C	
2. H		6. G	
3. A		7. A	
4. G		8. J	

Lesson 17
A

1. P, Mercury and Venus		5. S, moon	
2. P, planets		6. P, Scientists	
3. S, planet		7. S, year	
4. S, moon		8. S, Mercury	

Advantage Grammar Grade 3 © 2005 Creative Teaching Press

B
1. is
2. move
3. are
4. zoom
5. orbit
6. lies
7. measures
8. burn

C
Paragraphs will vary, but should show correct subject-verb agreement.

Lesson 18
A
1. are
2. Do
3. crash
4. are
5. Has
6. is
7. talk
8. is

B
1. correct
2. reflect
3. traps
4. correct
5. is
6. see
7. correct
8. do
9. are
10. Do

C
Paragraphs will vary, but should show correct subject-verb agreement.

Lesson 19
A
1. check
2.
3.
4. check
5. check
6.
7. check
8.
9. check
10.
11. check
12.

B (sample answers)
1. His favorite planet is Saturn.
2. Its name is the Roberts Museum of Space.
3. I would like to see the earth form space.
4. It is too dangerous.
5. My family went there last summer.

C
Sentences will vary but should all be accurate about the night sky and be complete, declarative sentences.

Lesson 20
A
1. check, add question mark
2.
3. check, add question mark
4. check, add question mark
5. check, add question mark
6. check, add question mark
7.
8.
9. check, add question mark
10.

B (sample answers)
1. What is Saturn?
2. What is Pluto?
3. What things make up the solar system?
4. What is a comet?
5. What are meteorites?

C
Questions will vary, but they should make sense and be complete interrogative sentences that end with question marks.

Lesson 21
A
1. sitting
2. C
3. flipped
4. swimmers
5. C
6. plugged
7. Winning
8. C
9. pinned
10. C

B
1. waiting
2. talking
3. C
4. C
5. C
6. slipped

C
1. spinning
2. batted
3. gagged
4. feeding
5. stomped
6. spitting

Lesson 22
A
1. A
2. They provide details that tell how the discovery of Uranus caused a stir.
3. indented

B
Paragraphs will vary. Students should provide supporting details that describe the excitement of space exploration.

Answer Key

Lesson 23
A
1. 5 and 7
2. indented
3. Books, movies, and TV programs show aliens.
4. Is there life on other planets?
5. looked

B
1. declarative; For example, no other planet has oxygen.
2. Animals on earth need oxygen to breathe
3. Any water on other planets is probably frozen.
4. How do oxygen and water affect life on other planets?
5. believed
6. D
7. sentence 11

Lesson 24
1. C	5. D
2. F	6. H
3. B	7. A
4. H	8. G

Lesson 25
A
1. We do not know exactly when Harriet Tubman was born.
2. Her place of birth was eastern Maryland.
3. Harriet Tubman's family lived on their owner's farm.
4. They worked in the farm fields.
5. Its main crop was tobacco.
6. Hers was a life filled with back-breaking work.
7. Gazing at the North Star, she dreamed.
8. It pointed the way toward the North and freedom.
9. My heart aches when I read about Harriet Tubman.
10. Yours would too.

B
1. Pers	5. Poss
2. Poss	6. Poss
3. Poss	7. Pers
4. Pers	8. Pers

C
Harriet liked to hear the older people tell stories. One old fellow seemed to know a lot. She listened in wonder to his tales of life in the North. "Ours is a hard life," he said. "But in the North, people are free, black and white. Children can go to school. No masters, no whips." Little Harriet wanted so badly to believe him. Their lives are so different from mine, she thought.

Lesson 26
A
1. Its	5. She
2. He	6. him
3. They	7. His
4. Their	8. It

B
1. Underline It, draw arrow from It to paper
2. Underline They, draw arrow from they to men
3. Underline them, draw arrow from them to rights
4. Underline Her, draw arrow from Her to Harriet
5. Underline theirs, draw arrow from theirs to slaves

C
Sentence pairs will vary. The second sentence should use a pronoun that agrees in person, number, and gender with the noun in the first sentence.

D
Sentence pairs will vary. The second sentence should use a pronoun that agrees in person, number, and gender with the noun in the first sentence.

Lesson 27
A
1. He went to the meeting on Saturday.
2. C
3. After the play, we talked about the Underground Railroad.
4. C
5. C
6. Gary showed me the program.
7. She goes to our school.
8. They go to a different school.
9. C
10. I can't think of anything right now.

B (sample answers)
1. She lived in Maryland.
2. It helped slaves to their freedom.
3. They sang "Go Down, Moses."
4. He was an old slave and friend to Harriet.
5. We read books and see films.

C
Sentences will vary but should correctly use the subject and object pronouns provided.

Lesson 28
A
1. One day, Harriet went to the town of Bucktown.
2. C
3. She visited a Quaker at her home.
4. Quakers helped slaves escape to free parts of the country.
5. C
6. The Quaker told Harriet to follow the Choptank River.
7. C
8. "The Underground Railroad goes through Camden," the woman said to Harriet.

B
Sentences will vary but should correctly capitalize the names of the geographical places.

Advantage Grammar Grade 3 © 2005 Creative Teaching Press

C
Paragraphs will vary but should correctly capitalize the names of the geographical places described.

Lesson 29
A

1. carries	11. fairies
2. babies	12. pays
3. marries	13. dairies
4. toys	14. enjoys
5. factories	15. copies
6. says	16. valleys
7. cities	17. obeys
8. glories	18. stories
9. joys	19. turkeys
10. monkeys	20. stays

B

1. valleys	6. Ferries
2. cities	7. boys
3. babies	8. blue jays
4. days	9. stories
5. bays	10. ways

C
Paragraphs will vary but should correctly add s to each word used when it becomes plural of third-person singular.

Lesson 30
A
Paragraphs will vary. They should, however, begin with a statement as a topic sentence and then support the statement with several relevant examples.

B
Paragraphs will vary. They should, however, begin with a topic sentence and then present details in correct sequential order.

Lesson 31
A
1. She settled in Philadelphia, Pennsylvania.
2. Pennsylvania
3. She washed clothes for fine ladies and gentlemen.
4. her
5. Her own family, and other people's families, still wore the chains of slavery.
6. she in sentence 11

B
1. time sequence order
2. Harriet Tubman rescued her brother and some others in a daring rescue.
3. It was Christmas time, and freezing rain filled the skies.
4. house in sentence 7
5. She knocked the secret knock.
6. The man snarled and said, "He was chased out of town! Now, get away from my house!"

Lesson 32

1. B		5. A	
2. F		6. G	
3. D		7. B	
4. F		8. H	

Lesson 33
A
1. Underline huge, draw arrow to baby
2. Underline eastern, draw arrow to state
3. Underline tall, draw arrow to trees
4. Underline small, draw arrow to East
5. Underline large, draw arrow to states
6. Underline gigantic, draw arrow to trees
7. Underline favorite, draw arrow to pet
8. Underline gentle, draw arrow to Babe
9. Underline strange, draw arrow to thing
10. Underline blue, draw arrow to Babe

B
Babe was an <u>amazing</u> animal. If a road was too <u>crooked</u> for hauling logs, Babe could fix that. Paul just hooked him up to the road and Babe pulled until it was <u>straight</u>. Babe caused some <u>big</u> problems, though. If he was <u>thirsty</u>, he could drink a <u>whole</u> river. Then the logs couldn't float. When Babe needed <u>new</u> shoes, there wasn't anywhere for him to lie down. Paul had to clear all of the Dakota Territory to make room!

C
Students' adjectives will vary but should be appropriate to the sentences.

Lesson 34
A
1. check, circle seven
2. check, circle hard
3. check, circle hungry
4.
5. check, circle big
6. check, circle special
7.
8. check, circle gigantic
9. check, circle large
10.

B
Sentences will vary but should correctly use the adjectives in appropriate sentences.

C
Paragraphs will vary but should correctly use some of the adjectives from the word box.

Lesson 35
A

1. check		7. check	
2. cities		8. check	
3.		9. check	
4.		10.	
5. check		11.	
6.		12. check	

Answer Key

B (sample answers)
1. Hurry up with those pancakes.
2. Get out of the flower bed, Babe!
3. Please chop a tall one, Paul.
4. Babe, put your shoes back on.
5. Don't step on our house, Paul.
6. Light a fire, Paul.
7. Babe, sit!
8. Please get me that video form the library.
9. Leave a few trees standing.
10. Don't tell me any more stories about Paul and Babe.

Lesson 36
A
1. C
2. How to Be a Logger
3. The History of Axes
4. Favorite Songs of America's Lumberjacks
5. Life in the North Woods of Canada
6. C
7. A Guide to Raising Oxen
8. 1000 Favorite Recipes for Pancakes
9. C
10. Born in Maine, Raised in Minnesota

B (sample answers)
1. A Guide to Shoeing Oxen
2. How to Get the Lumberjack Look
3. Minnesota, the Gopher State
4. What to Look for When Buying an Axe
5. Which Tree Is That?
6. Ships of the Great Lakes

C
E-mails will vary but should correctly capitalize the titles of the books.

Lesson 37
A
1. new
2. hole
3. C
4. by
5. there
6. hear
7. C
8. guest
9. C
10. whole

B (sample answers)
1. This football didn't cost me a cent!
2. We saw a deer drinking from the stream.
3. I think I will dye my hair green.
4. Did you send the package by first class mail?
5. I like my toast buttered, but Dad likes it plain.
6. Looking for the lost needle is a waste of time.

Lesson 38
A
Paragraphs will vary. They should, however, begin with a cause as a topic sentence and then give several effects of the cause
B
Paragraphs will vary. They should, however, begin with an effect as a topic sentence and then list several causes of the effect.

Lesson 39
A
1. tall, young, tough, ornery
2. Guess what happened when Bill's friend tried to ride Widow Maker.
3. sample answer: A worried Bill tried to talk his friend out of trying to ride Widow Maker.
4. The rider thought he was doing all right.
5. sentence 1

B
6. cause and effect
7. the cause of the effects that follow
8. He shot up into the clear blue sky.
9. tasty, green, big, crazy
10. sample answer: He gave a mighty yank and pulled the man back down.

Lesson 40
1. B
2. F
3. D
4. H
5. A
6. J
7. D
8. G

Lesson 41
A
1. bedroom. N
2. good-looking A
3. dark-colored A
4. fireworks N
5. Thanksgiving N
6. cardboard N
7. homework N
8. Evergreen A
9. graveyards N
10. textbook N

B
Students' sentences will vary but should use the compound word appropriately.

C
1. grandfather
2. silverware
3. underwater
4. iceberg
5. barefoot

Advantage Grammar Grade 3 © 2005 Creative Teaching Press

Lesson 42

A
1.
2.
3. check, add !
4.
5. check, add !
6.
7.
8. check, add !
9. check, add !
10.
11.
12. check, add !

B (sample answers)
1. Watch your sleeve!
2. Hurry up, the parade's beginning!
3. Hey, you scared me!
4. Boy, am I full!
5. Yes! Only three more days of school!

C
Paragraphs will vary but should contain at least one correct exclamatory sentence.

Lesson 43

A
1. In what month do we celebrate Father's Day?
2. C
3. It's the samba-dancing holiday known as Carnival.
4. Japan celebrates a holiday called Children's Day on My 5 each year.
5. C
6. Jewish children dress up in costumes for Purim, which takes place in late winter.

B
Answers will vary but should use correct capitalization when writing the name of a holiday. Suggested holidays:
1. Birthdays, Hanukkah, Christmas, St. Lucia, Trung Thu, Halloween, Diwali
2. Carnival, Purim, N'cwala, Holi, Mother's Day, Easter, Passover
3. Christmas, Independence Day, Mother's or Father's Day
4. almost any holiday
5. In the United States, Memorial Day, Flag Day, Independence Day, Veteran's Day; national holidays in other countries will vary.

C
Paragraphs will vary but should use correct capitalization when naming holidays.

Lesson 44

A
1. C
2. It started in 1776 at the Battle of Lexington.
3. It is also called the War of Independence.
4. C
5. It was the turning point of the Civil War.
6. That war took place in the Nineteenth Century.
7. Dad's grandfather lived during the Great Depression.
8. That was before the Second World War.

B
1. Sunday
2. July
3. Answers will vary but should be capitalized.
4. June
5. Thursday
6. April
7. Tuesday
8. Answers will vary but should be capitalized.
9. October
10. Answers will vary but should be capitalized.

Lesson 45

A
Paragraphs will vary but should make relevant comparisons and contrasts between the two holidays.

B
Paragraphs will vary but should make relevant comparisons between the two holidays.

C
Paragraphs will vary but should make relevant contrasts between the two holidays.

Lesson 46

A
1. correct order: costume, Halloween, mask
2. correct order: firecracker, Fourth, parade
3. check
4. correct order: fabulous, father, morning, mother
5. correct order: new, noisemaker, party, popcorn
6. check

B
correct order: candy, card, celebrate, colorful, cookies, family, firecracker, flag, flowers, gift, give, light, noise, parade, pie, pumpkin, remember, rose, treat, trick

C
Words will vary but list should be in correct alphabetical order.

Answer Key

Lesson 47

A
1. evergreen, sometimes, candlelight
2. sentence 1
3. Some Saint Lucia crowns have real candles, others have electric candles.
4. It takes place on December 13, one of the longest, darkest nights in Sweden.
5. crown, elected, holiday, honors, longest, middle, real, red, school, white

B
1. sentences 10 and 14
2. sentence 4, best-known, and sentence 8, extra-thin
3. It comes 12 days before Christmas and helps start the holiday season.
4. the two kinds of cookies, the Lucia buns and the ginger snaps
5. saffron, saint, season, sings, snaps, song, special, spice, story, summer

Lesson 48
1. C   5. B
2. F   6. F
3. C   7. A
4. J   8. J

Practice Test
1. B
2. H
3. A
4. H
5. B
6. J
7. C
8. G
9. B
10. F
11. D
12. G
13. B
14. H
15. D
16. J
17. C
18. F
19. A
20. G
21. A
22. H
23. D
24. J

Advantage Grammar Grade 3 © 2005 Creative Teaching Press